MURDER *in* WAUWATOSA

THE MYSTERIOUS DEATH OF BUDDY SCHUMACHER

PAUL HOFFMAN

THE History PRESS

Published by The History Press
Charleston, SC 29403
www.historypress.net

Cover images: All Schumacher family photos courtesy of Brian Egloff and Keith Egloff. Recent photos of Wauwatosa by Paul Hoffman.

First published 2012

Manufactured in the United States

ISBN 978.1.60949.673.9

Library of Congress Cataloging-in-Publication Data

Hoffman, Paul, 1963-
Murder in Wauwatosa : the mysterious death of Buddy Schumacher / Paul Hoffman.
p. cm.
ISBN 978-1-60949-673-9
1. Schumacher, Arthur. 2. Murder--Wisconsin--Wauwatosa. 3. Murder--Investigation--Wisconsin--Wauwatosa. I. Title.
HV6534.W38H64 2012
364.152'30977594--dc23
2012022157

Notice: The information in this book is true and complete to the best of our knowledge. It is offered without guarantee on the part of the author or The History Press. The author and The History Press disclaim all liability in connection with the use of this book.

For Brian, Keith and Gordon.

CONTENTS

ACKNOWLEDGEMENTS

I would like to thank the following: my wonderful wife, Kimberly, who has been with me and encouraged me through all the investigation, writing and editing of this book; my awesome daughters, Kirsten, Jaclyn and Emily, who gave up a little bit of Daddy time during this process; my father and mother, Raymond and Sharon Hoffman, for their love, encouragement and pride; my brothers, Mark, Douglas and Andrew Hoffman, for all those things that brothers do; Brian Egloff, Keith Egloff and Gordon Schumacher for sharing memories, photographs and research of their family with me; Ben Gibson and the staff at The History Press for all their hard work and having faith in me as an author and in this story as book-worthy; Robert Tanzillo, a fellow author who suggested that I contact The History Press and pitch my idea; Karen Barry and the Wauwatosa Historical Society staff for their tremendous support and help; the staff at *Wauwatosa NOW* for publishing my three-part series on this subject in 2010; David R. Windisch Jr., who helped with the preparation of many of the photographs herein and whose daily taunting has actually become enjoyable; authors Michael John Sullivan and Heather Hummel for their advice and encouragement; Olive Crawford, former English teacher at Wauwatosa East High School, who instilled in me a desire to learn and employ proper English grammar and usage; Ryan Felton, who advised me to see one project through to completion before moving on to another; Larry Widen, whose photo services saved me loads of time when he noticed my wife and I taking notes from old *Wauwatosa News* articles with pencil and paper; friends, supporters, teachers, coaches and bosses too numerous to mention by name (if you're not sure, just go ahead and include yourself); Art Schumacher for selling his house to my dad in 1969; and finally Lillian Harwood for sparking my interest in "the Schumacher boy," leading me on a forty-year odyssey to tell Buddy's story.

Chapter 1

MRS. HARWOOD KNOWS

I know who killed the Schumacher boy.
–Lillian Harwood

Lillian Harwood lived with her husband, James, next door to my family for several years when I was growing up in Wauwatosa, Wisconsin, a suburb just west of Milwaukee. Mrs. Harwood was generally a good-natured older lady who served as a school crossing guard at the corner of Milwaukee and Wauwatosa Avenues between Wauwatosa East High School and Lincoln Elementary.

She loved kids and enjoyed gregariously telling me and my three younger brothers to "make all the noise you want!" or "You're one of the good ones!"

There were times, though, when Mrs. Harwood did or said things that kind of made you scratch your head. These days, we would say that she might have been getting Alzheimer's. Back in the 1970s, we just thought she was kind of crazy—usually a harmless, odd type of crazy, but crazy nonetheless.

She once washed her car with a garden hose…the inside of her car. When a basketball accidentally got tipped over the fence from our driveway basketball court into her backyard and my brothers or I went to her back door to ask if we could retrieve the ball, we were never quite sure which Mrs. Harwood would answer the door. More often than not, it was the one who was happy to see children at her door. Sometimes she wasn't quite so together. Once, when my brothers went over, they heard the rock band Foreigner's "Head Games" blaring from her kitchen radio. Mrs. Harwood asked them if they liked the pretty Christmas music. Crazy, but harmless crazy.

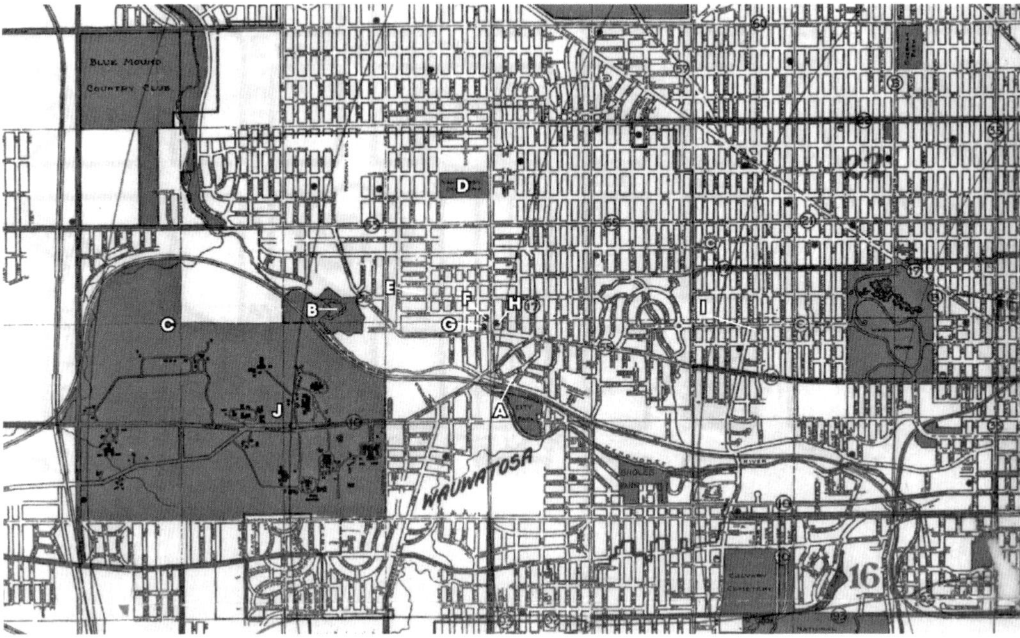

A map of key locations in the Buddy Schumacher story on the 1930 *Caspar's Official Map of the City of Milwaukee & Vicinity. Copyright C.N. Caspar Company. Permission sought.*

A: The Schumacher home, 191 Alice Street, which later became 1319 Alice Street and then 1319 Seventy-fourth Street. The site is now a parking lot.
B: The island in the Menomonee River near which there was a swimming hole called Blackridge.
C: The approximate location where the body was found.
D: Wauwatosa Cemetery, where Buddy was buried.
E: Originally 176 West Center Street, and now 8118 Hillcrest Drive, the house to which the Schumacher family moved in 1927.
F: Lincoln Elementary School.
G: Longfellow Junior High School, which is now at the corner of North and Wauwatosa Avenues, just south of the Wauwatosa Cemetery.
H: Wauwatosa High School, now Wauwatosa East.
I: Mount Olive Lutheran Church, 5327 West Washington Boulevard, Milwaukee, where the Schumachers attended.
J: An area of several hospitals, including the Milwaukee Sanitarium/Psychiatric Hospital (later the Dewey Center and now the Aurora Psychiatric Hospital), Muirdale Sanitorium, Milwaukee County Home for Dependent Children, the Milwaukee County Infirmary (originally known as the Almshouse and was torn down in the 1970s) and the Milwaukee County Insane Asylum.

However, there were also these rare times when, as a young boy, I felt like I needed to keep my distance. Mrs. Harwood would occasionally slowly patrol the sidewalk in front of her house on the 8100 block of

Hillcrest Drive with flushed cheeks and an intense glare in her eyes. She would eyeball every car parked on the street that she didn't recognize and look us in the eye, saying things like, "They look in my windows at night" or, "I know who killed the Schumacher boy."

Over the course of a few years, Mrs. Harwood told me that the police knew who killed the Schumacher boy and that it happened near the Menomonee River and the railroad tracks around Hoyt Park. When I was about ten or twelve years old or so and heard her say things like this, I mostly chalked it up to her being an old lady who either misinterpreted things she'd seen or heard or was being paranoid and crazy…or both. But the statements she made about the Schumacher boy started me wondering—my father had bought our house at 8118 Hillcrest Drive in 1969 from a man named Art Schumacher.

I started asking myself a lot of questions. Did Mr. Schumacher have a brother or a son who was killed? If so, did the police know who killed him? Was Mrs. Harwood insinuating that there had been some sort of coverup? Was this just some figment of her imagination, or did she really know who killed the boy?

I asked my dad, and he said he didn't know if Art Schumacher had a brother or son at all, much less one who had been killed. Being a young kid, I was too unnerved by Mrs. Harwood's demeanor when she mentioned "the Schumacher boy" that I never asked her for any more information. I'd just mumble an "uh huh" and go about my business.

I kept going about my business for the next thirty-five years or so. I got married and had kids, and through it all, every now and then, thoughts of "the Schumacher boy" (if there ever really was such a boy) would creep into my head.

Around Christmastime in 2009, when I was visiting my parents' new home in Brookfield, I finally decided to find out once and for all if anything Mrs. Harwood said about this boy was true. An online search produced a photo published in the September 16, 1925 *Milwaukee Sentinel* of a casket being carried out of a Wauwatosa house. A headline above the photo read "BID SCHUMACHER BOY FAREWELL," and the photo caption read in part, "Arthur (Buddie) Schumacher, murder victim, leaving his home on Alice Street, Wauwatosa, for the last time after funeral services yesterday."

Oh my gosh! There really *was* a Schumacher boy who was killed. The accompanying story shed little light on the circumstances of the boy's death. But the more I dug, the more I found out just how much of what Mrs. Harwood said about the Schumacher boy was indeed true, or at least how some people could have come to some of the same conclusions that she had.

Chapter 2

MEDIA COVERAGE

Arthur Schumacher Jr., an eight-year-old boy with a sunny disposition and a kind heart, left his home near what is today Seventy-fourth and State Streets in Wauwatosa on a warm morning in late July 1925, eagerly anticipating the fun he'd have with some friends at the local swimming hole called Blackridge just outside town. But the next time the boy (known to almost everyone as "Buddy") came home was seven weeks later in a casket. He'd been sexually abused and killed when someone suffocated him by stuffing a handkerchief far down his throat.

The killing was considered so unusual and horrifying that Wauwatosa's weekly newspaper, the *Wauwatosa News*, noted in an August 6, 1925 article that it evoked memories of a case more than fifty years earlier from Pennsylvania. Buddy's case was thought to be the first child sex killing in sixteen years in the Milwaukee area and only one of four through the first fifty-eight years of the 1900s, a 1959 *Milwaukee Sentinel* article reported.

Even though a local vagrant was arrested in connection with the crime shortly after Buddy's body was found, and though two other men later confessed to the killing, nobody ever faced charges in the case. Several incidents during the investigation leave one confounded. Among them, witnesses changed their minds about key pieces of evidence against the vagrant, the handkerchief used to suffocate the boy was unable to be located in the district attorney's office for a few days and neither of the confessions were initially believed by police.

The Wauwatosa Police Department, which would have had files on the case at one time, no longer has any records for years prior to 1934, according to a department spokesperson. And nearly everyone who was connected with the case has now died. Very few of the descendants of the people involved in the mystery were told much about it. While plenty of information was available on the Schumacher family through family members, the main sources of information on this case and on the other people involved were census records, prison records and newspaper articles.

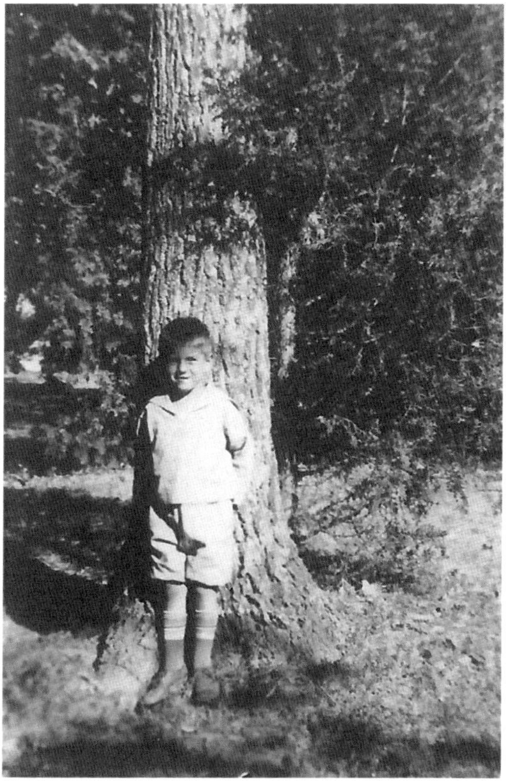

Buddy Schumacher, four years old.

Because local newspapers' accounts of some of the happenings in this case conflicted, one needs to understand the news coverage philosophies of those papers at that time in order to get as close to the facts as we can get. This story played out intensely in the local newspapers: the big city daily papers in Milwaukee (the *Sentinel* and the *Journal*) and Wauwatosa's weekly newspaper (the *Wauwatosa News*). Coverage in the Milwaukee papers was sometimes fairly sensationalistic.

The Milwaukee papers had been engaged in a constant state of fierce competition for many years, and they would continue to be in such a state for years to come. By the time of the Schumacher crime, the "yellow journalism" scourge of the turn of the century had faded somewhat.

Yellow journalism, according to American historian and journalist Frank Luther Mott, was characterized by scare headlines in huge print, often of minor news; lavish use of pictures or imaginary drawings; use of faked interviews, misleading headlines, pseudoscience and a parade of false learning from so-called experts; and dramatic sympathy, with the "underdog" pitted against the system.

These kinds of reporting and story presentation have often been connected to supermarket tabloids through the years. They largely disappeared in reputable newspapers as the twentieth century pressed on. But in 1925,

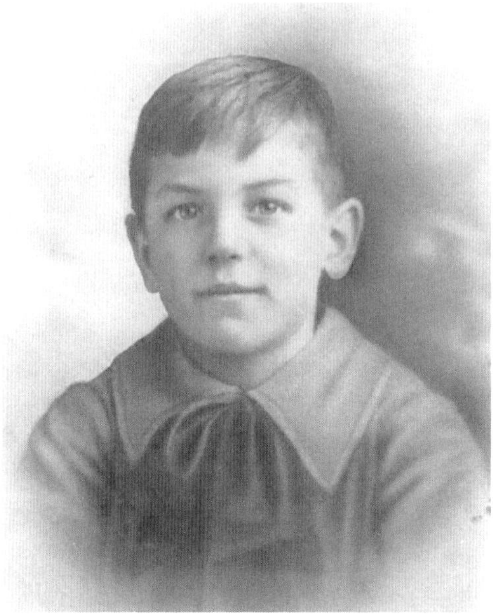

Buddy Schumacher, six years old.

elements of yellow journalism sometimes still existed.

Milwaukee was no exception, and at the time, the *Sentinel* seemed to be a bit "yellower" than the *Journal*. That shouldn't come as much of a surprise since the *Sentinel* had been purchased the previous year by the Hearst Corporation, whose founder, William Randolph Hearst, played a key role at the peak of yellow journalism and whose life served as one of the inspirations for the title character in Orson Welles's *Citizen Kane*.

When covering the Buddy Schumacher story, both Milwaukee papers often splashed huge headlines across the tops of their front pages. Both printed photos that reputable papers today would never consider publishing. It seemed that some of the "facts" got trumped up a bit, too, and reporters went to measures that would have been unheard of a few decades later. Brian Egloff, Buddy's nephew who lived in Wauwatosa for a time in the 1940s and lives in Australia now, said that he had been told that reporters clambered over the fences at the Schumacher home to get photos and interviews with the family after the boy disappeared.

The *Wauwatosa News*, on the other hand, provided its readers with much more toned-down coverage of the saga. The stories contained the basic facts, but the headlines were much, much smaller, there were not nearly so many quotes in the stories and the *News* printed only one photo during the entirety of its coverage: a head-and-shoulders shot of Buddy published two weeks after he went missing.

The *Wauwatosa News* publisher at the time was Cornelius L. Benoy, who lived just up Alice Street from the Schumachers. The paper had been owned by either Cornelius or his father, John Benoy, since 1907, and Cornelius would continue to serve as publisher and/or editor until the early 1940s. With Buddy's grandfather, John Armstrong, having been one of the town's business and political leaders in the early part of the 1900s, the Benoys surely knew the family.

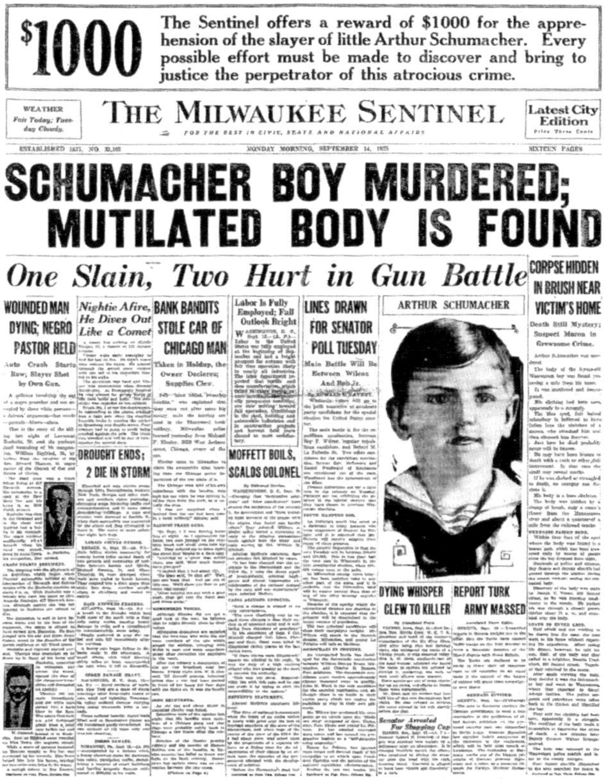

$1000 The Sentinel offers a reward of $1000 for the apprehension of the slayer of little Arthur Schumacher. Every possible effort must be made to discover and bring to justice the perpetrator of this atrocious crime.

THE MILWAUKEE SENTINEL

Latest City Edition

MONDAY MORNING, SEPTEMBER 14, 1925

SIXTEEN PAGES

SCHUMACHER BOY MURDERED; MUTILATED BODY IS FOUND

One Slain, Two Hurt in Gun Battle

CORPSE HIDDEN IN BRUSH NEAR VICTIM'S HOME

WOUNDED MAN DYING; NEGRO PASTOR HELD

Nightie Afire, He Dives Out Like a Comet

BANK BANDITS STOLE CAR OF CHICAGO MAN

Labor Is Fully Employed; Fall Outlook Bright

LINES DRAWN FOR SENATOR POLL TUESDAY

ARTHUR SCHUMACHER

DROUGHT ENDS; 2 DIE IN STORM

MOFFETT BOILS, SCALDS COLONEL

DYING WHISPER CLEW TO KILLER

REPORT TURK ARMY MASSED

"Schumacher Boy Murdered; Mutilated Body Is Found," *Milwaukee Sentinel*, September 14, 1925.

The Benoys were said to be extremely committed to their town. John Benoy, a printer who moved to Wauwatosa in 1895, had newspaper experience at all three of Milwaukee's big daily papers (*Sentinel*, *Journal* and *Evening Wisconsin*) before taking a job with L.R. Gridley, founder of the *Wauwatosa News*. He bought out Gridley's interest in 1907 and became editor and sole proprietor.

In *Memoirs of Milwaukee County*, published in 1909, John Benoy was described as

> *a strong, independent and conscientious man, an excellent type of citizen, and a desirable addition to the editorial ranks of the country, in the present era, when there seems to be a superfluous amount of "yellow journalism."*
>
> *He brings to his work the practical experience of the printer, and a familiarity with the methods of the city papers, as well as those sterling qualities of character which are the most important factors of success in the important work of the journalist.*

His son was similarly described in *History of Milwaukee City and County*, published in 1922. Cornelius Benoy, or C.L., as some called him, had just taken over as editor and sole proprietor of the *Wauwatosa News* from his father the year before. Cornelius's professional attributes were described thusly in *History of Milwaukee*: "He has made it a live interesting journal, devoted to the welfare of the community." And of his character, it was said that "[h]e is favorably known among a constantly broadening circle of friends and is regarded as one of the stalwart champions of the community in which he makes his home."

Cornelius Benoy was five years old when his family moved to "Tosa," so this was his hometown. He worked in the *News*' printing office for six years and helped found a newspaper in Centerville, Illinois, before returning.

The Schumacher coverage was one example of how the *Wauwatosa News* seemed to protect its townspeople and officials.

Another example of the *News*' protective nature can be found in an apology that the *News*' editor printed in an October 1932 edition. The apology came down hard on a reporter who had omitted two women's names from a list of a company's attachés. The editor went extremely overboard in stating his displeasure with his reporter's faux pas: "The chagrin and mortification of the editor when he received a belated notification that these charming young ladies had been overlooked and ignored can be better imagined than described."

The editor then called the offending reporter a "miscreant" and said that he'd been "called on the carpet" and fired. Whether he would ever be allowed to work for the *Wauwatosa News* again would depend on his behavior over the winter.

Considering its protective leanings toward its town and citizens, and the fact that the Benoys also must have known the Schumachers and Armstrongs, it's understandable that the local newspaper treated Buddy's case with kid gloves.

But the Buddy Schumacher story is more than just a "whodunit" murder mystery. It's also a story of how a father and mother tried to cope with a missing boy whom they eventually found out had been molested and murdered. It's a story of the state of mental healthcare in the 1920s and the vagabond lifestyle of the day, one in which many men—some of whom were mentally challenged—traveled from one place to another looking for handouts.

And while the story of Buddy Schumacher's death may be a tragic one, some good did come of it as city officials started the process of making their city safer.

Chapter 3

THE SCHUMACHERS

Buddy Schumacher's parents—Art and Florence—came from quite different family backgrounds. Both families were among the wave of European immigrants coming to America in the second half of the nineteenth century. A great-grandfather, Fredrich Schumacher, emigrated from Pomerania, a province of Prussia on the Baltic Sea that is now split between Poland and Germany, and settled in New York before coming to Wisconsin. Buddy's maternal grandfather, John Armstrong, came to Milwaukee from Ireland and made a good deal of money in horseshoeing and real estate.

The Schumacher family was a tightly knit, fairly poor Lutheran clan, but Art somehow ended up marrying into one of the top merchant families in Wauwatosa. Perhaps Art took the cue from his own father, who married into one of Milwaukee's most prominent families. Louis Schumacher had married Eliza Pritzlaff, niece of famous Milwaukee hardware merchant John Pritzlaff.

"That is what is so amazing," Brian Egloff marveled. "How did this very rich man's daughter marry a Schumacher, virtually a penniless parochial schoolteacher?"

Louis eventually lost all the money Eliza had inherited, partially due to caring for his ill wife late in life. But perhaps it was his mother and father's marriage that contributed to Art's understanding of how to become accepted by the wealthy and powerful—and perhaps spurred the local business community to get so involved in the search for his son.

The Schumacher household Art grew up in was very frugal and hardworking, according to Brian Egloff. Art was an apprentice watchmaker

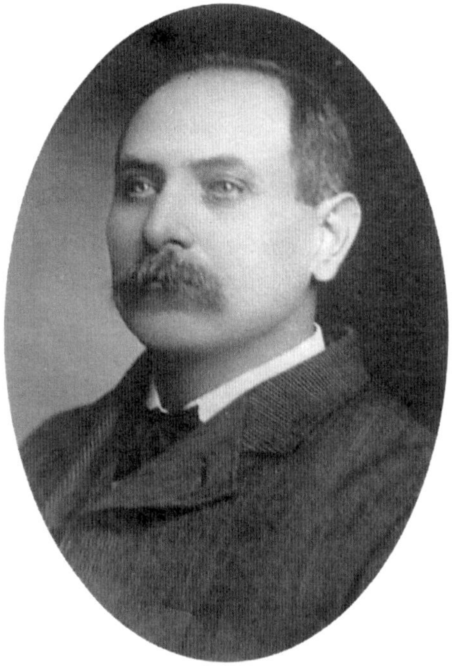

John Armstrong, Buddy Schumacher's maternal grandfather, was an Irish immigrant who held a great deal of political and financial clout in Wauwatosa and Milwaukee County in the early 1900s.

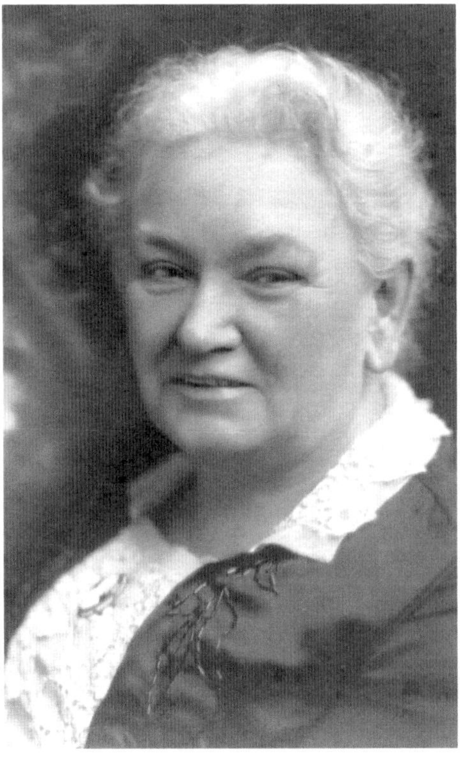

Alice Regina Hundhausen Armstrong, John Armstrong's wife.

by the time he was twelve years old and wound up selling surgical instruments for the E.H. Karrer Company, owned by Eduard Karrer, a man Art attended church with at Mount Olive Lutheran on Washington Boulevard on the far west side of Milwaukee. Art rose to the position of assistant manager with the firm.

The Armstrong side presented quite a contrast to the Schumacher side of Buddy's ancestry. The Armstrongs had a solid record of financial success and political clout in Milwaukee and Wauwatosa in the early 1900s. Not only was John Armstrong successful, but his wife, Alice, came from a prosperous family herself. Alice's grandfather, Frederick William Hundhausen, a Prussian immigrant, was a doctor, saloon owner, school administrator and city treasurer in Milwaukee after serving in the Union army as a quartermaster during the Civil War.

John and Alice moved from Milwaukee to Wauwatosa sometime in the late 1880s. By 1892, according to the Wauwatosa city directory of that year, the Armstrongs were established at the northwest corner of what was then Alice Street and Watertown Plank Road (later to become Seventy-fourth and State Streets) near what is now a George Webb restaurant. This building also served as Armstrong's blacksmith shop. Eventually, the family moved out of the blacksmith shop building and into a house one property north, at 191 Alice Street. The house was torn down many years ago, and a parking lot stands there now.

It wasn't long after moving to Tosa that John Armstrong was recognized as one of the town's top business leaders. He lost three buildings in Tosa's Great Fire of 1895, among the three hardest-hit businessmen in the blaze. This fire, suspected to be an arson, decimated the downtown business district, including Armstrong's buildings that housed a barbershop, a saloon and a harness shop. It was estimated that Armstrong's losses totaled $3,000, according to a *Milwaukee Journal* story of July 10, 1895. That is about $75,000 in today's money.

Armstrong's political clout in town and in Milwaukee County was similarly expansive. He was Wauwatosa's representative on the Milwaukee County Board of Supervisors while Wauwatosa was still a village. In 1896, he was given the chairmanship of the county insane asylum. When Wauwatosa was incorporated as a city in 1897, Armstrong was elected to represent one of the city's four wards on the county council. He continued to serve Wauwatosa and Milwaukee County as a supervisor and/or common council member through 1908, with the exception of 1904–5. He was also the city assessor for a time.

His wife was a noted businesswoman herself, owning various properties in and around Wauwatosa. She was also a member of the Wauwatosa Women's Club, founded in 1894. The city honored her by naming the street the family lived on Alice Street.

While the Schumachers tended to be low-key, spiritually minded folks, the Armstrong clan of the day tended to be more boisterous, bigger drinkers and maybe not quite as god-fearing, Brian Egloff said. The cause of death listed on John Armstrong's death certificate was cirrhosis of the liver, which quite likely indicated heavy alcohol consumption.

The Schumachers got together often for large family gatherings, although these gatherings generally consisted of church family members rather than relatives. The family was very committed to their church, and Art and Florence's children, Buddy and Jeanette (later picking up the nickname "Netzy" from her husband), attended Sunday school at Mount Olive.

"In general, German Lutherans are stoic, accepting whatever comes their way, and are not fearful because they have faith in God," said Keith Egloff, Brian's brother who lives in Virginia. "They tend to have a subdued, almost dry sense of humor. As Art and Netzy aged, I believed that they laughed and giggled more."

Brian Egloff said that there was little alcohol consumption among Schumacher family members, especially in public view. But a big deal was not made out of it either way. "I didn't get an idea any of the Schumachers drank a lot," Egloff said. "I got an idea they lived in god-fearing moderation. At family gatherings, alcohol was never a feature, neither its presence nor it absence. They might have had a beer or they might have not. My grandfather might have had wine, but it was so small an amount as to almost not notice."

The Armstrongs were a different breed. "I never got the idea they were particularly keen on church," Brian Egloff said. "That side of the family didn't tend to have big family gatherings like the Schumacher family did."

Perhaps it was partially due to his political offices that he could be seen as a target at times, but John Armstrong was involved in some newsworthy incidents in the 1890s and early 1900s. In June 1897, he was accused of assaulting a Wauwatosa constable, Julius Marquardt. A story in the July 1, 1897 *Milwaukee Journal* noted that Armstrong was alleged to have been "conducting himself in a disorderly manner in front of the Lefeber Bros. store in Wauwatosa when the marshal threatened to arrest him. Mr. Armstrong took offense, and, it is said, assaulted the marshal." Armstrong was later acquitted.

Later that year, as a member of the Milwaukee County Board, Armstrong was reported to have helped a former supervisor exact revenge on a rival by

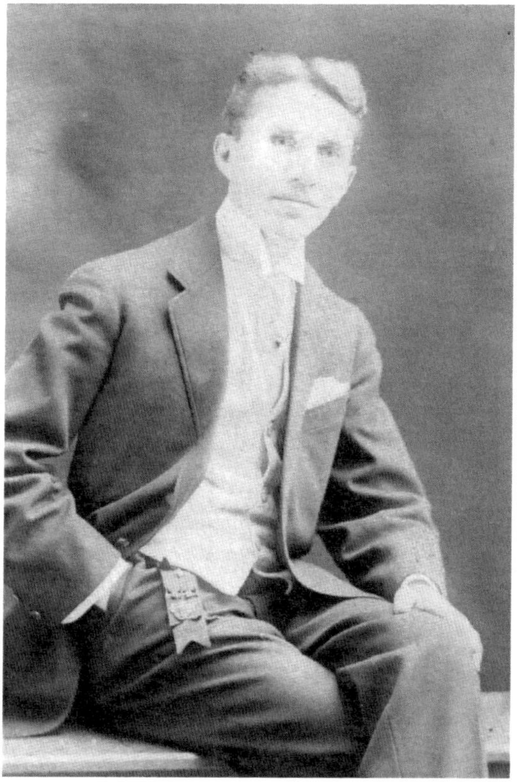

Buddy's father, Art Schumacher, 1910.

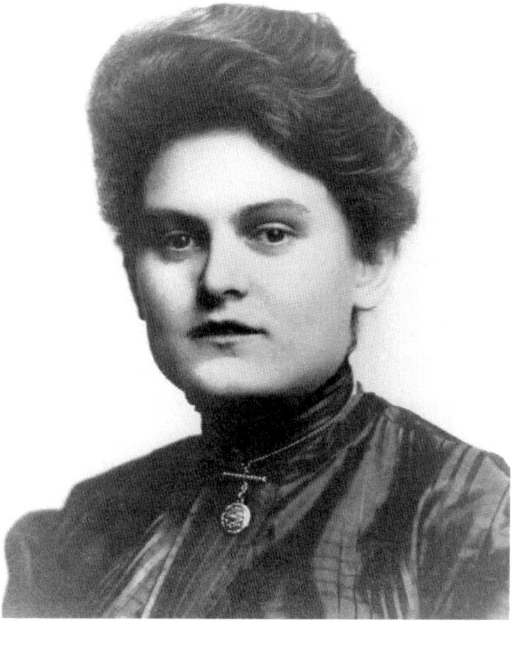

Florence May Zapp Armstrong Schumacher, Buddy's mother.

changing his vote after the roll call had been taken on a vote for the county's superintendent of city poor. Eight years later, Armstrong was one of twenty-four Milwaukee County supervisors or ex-supervisors indicted on bribery charges. He faced five counts of accepting between $50 and $100 to give contracts to plumbers and others for bonuses, according to a July 17, 1905 story in the *Racine Daily Journal.*

These incidents involving John Armstrong may shed a little light on the political arena of the late 1800s and early 1900s in Milwaukee County, as well as on Armstrong's notoriety and the potential to have developed some enemies.

Florence May Zapp Armstrong, Buddy's mother, was the second oldest of the seven surviving children of John and Alice Armstrong, and some of the boys in the family were said to be "a bit wild," Brian Egloff said.

Florence did enjoy playing with her younger brothers, though, and was a big sports enthusiast, especially enjoying the old minor-league Milwaukee Brewers and, later on, the major-league Milwaukee Braves games on the radio with her husband. And boy, did she get excited when her team won! It was the playful nature she exhibited with her brothers that led to Art calling her "Sis."

"Grandmother was an exceptionally warm and caring person who never said a bad word about anyone," recalled Brian Egloff.

Keith Egloff described his grandparents, Art and Florence, in great detail years later:

> *She* [Florence] *was always willing to play simple card games with me (War, Go Fish, etc.) and tiddlywinks on the kitchen table. I remember their 50th wedding anniversary. It was a big party in a large building. Arthur sang with his barbershop quartet (the Mellow Fellows), which was the only time that I heard him sing with the group. They had straw hats and wooden canes. I still have one of his canes.*
>
> *Arthur, or Art, was always thin and in good health, and Jeanette remembers him always as being bald. At some point in his life he got hit in the nose by a golf ball that crossed over from the adjacent fairway. After that his nose was always large.*
>
> *He also had a very bad ear infection, and the doctors had to drill through his skull near his mastoid process to remove the infection, thereby ending his hearing out of one ear.*
>
> *I remember as a young boy Arthur hitting me baseballs straight up in the air with a bat. For his age, he could really hit the ball. He also showed me and* [my brother] *Jerry how to juggle balls, saying that it was a good way to gain eye-hand coordination.*

Arthur loved to play cards, particularly Sheepshead, or Schafkopf. Arthur played Sheepshead right up until he died. Arthur, as did most people, counted cards during each hand, so that he knew what cards were left, and by the way people played their cards, he knew who had which cards.

I remember going to large family picnics in a park, the kids and younger adults playing baseball and the older adults playing cards on tables. Of course, there was always beer drinking. Arthur always liked to have a beer. He would nurse it along and savor it, and probably seldom had more that one.

Arthur was a very detailed person and very fastidious. He repaired watches and clocks when he was young and the family still has a number of watches and clocks that he got early in life. He always dressed well—white shirt, hat, and often with a tie.

There was never a dandelion or weed in his lawn or garden. He would carefully unwrap a gift and rewrap it so that it looked as if it never had been opened.

He worked in a drug store and did a little of everything. Early on he did watch repair, later he did simple medical procedures (lance boils, etc.), and he also ordered medical supplies and medicines.

He kept a stamp collection. The stamps he got off letters and packages which he received from ordering/communicating with companies in other countries. He did daily exercises and his mind was sharp almost right up until he died at the Lutheran Home in Wauwatosa.

Art and Florence married on August 10, 1909, in Wauwatosa. Nearly six years later, on April 11, 1915, their first child was born, a girl named Jeanette Alice. Less than two years later, their second and last child, Arthur Louis Schumacher Jr. ("Buddy"), was born on September 2, 1916.

The whole family got sick, and Art nearly died, during the influenza epidemic of 1918, according to Gordon Schumacher, Art's nephew and a cousin of the Egloff brothers. The epidemic killed more than 50 million people worldwide, more deaths than in all of World War I. By that time, John Armstrong had died and his wife had moved to the country near North Prairie with her oldest daughter, Gertrude, and Gertrude's husband, Charles Brown.

"The house was cold and dark," Gordon Schumacher said of Art and Florence's home during the time of the epidemic, "and it was Grandmother Armstrong who came in from the North Prairie farm and got the food and the house going again."

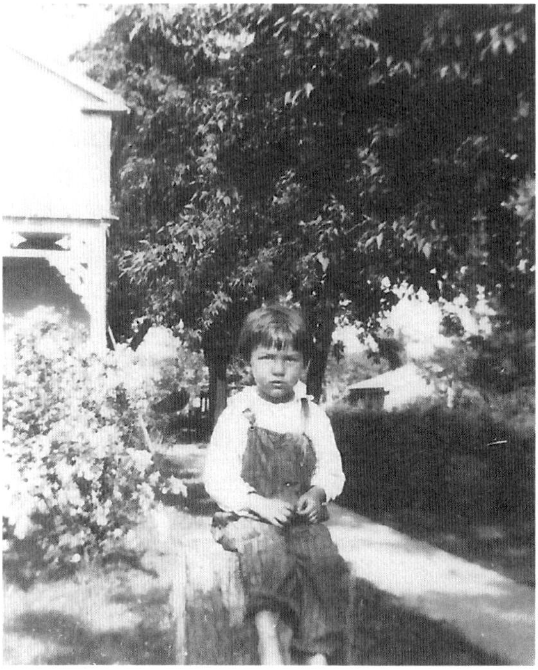

Buddy Schumacher at his Aunt Gert and Uncle Charles Brown's house in North Prairie.

In the fall of 1921, Art and Florence enrolled both Buddy and Jeanette in Lincoln Elementary School, with Buddy in kindergarten and his sister in second grade. Buddy also attended Washington School for a time, according to records supplied by Lincoln School, while his sister remained at Lincoln.

The Washington School neighborhood is about a mile or so northeast of the bustling downtown business area of Wauwatosa, called "the Village." Lincoln, on the other hand, is just a few blocks due north of the Village.

The Schumachers lived in two different houses in Wauwatosa before eventually moving into the Armstrong house to share it with some of Florence's brothers, perhaps not the best location for young children to hang out at that time.

Chapter 4

WAUWATOSA IN THE 1920S

The 1920s were a time of sweeping change in the United States, and Wauwatosa was not immune to some of those changes.

Advances in the first twenty years of the new century, such as movies, radio and popular magazines, created movie and sports stars who represented a glamorous new age. But besides the glamour that youngsters emulated, there were also practices such as smoking, bad language, immorality and selfishness that some mimicked, too.

One of the biggest agents of change during this decade was the "noble experiment" of prohibition. Signed in 1919, it made the manufacture, transportation, import, export and sale of alcoholic beverages restricted or illegal. Prohibition was supposed to lower crime and corruption, reduce social problems, lower taxes needed to support prisons and poorhouses and improve health and hygiene in America. Instead, alcohol became more dangerous to consume, organized crime blossomed, courts and prison systems became overloaded and endemic corruption of police and public officials occurred.

The Milwaukee area may have had a more difficult time adjusting to prohibition than many other places in the country, and the act was considered detrimental to the cultural character of the city, notes the Milwaukee County Historical Society on its website. Milwaukee was long known for its many breweries, as well as its large German population, which enjoyed its beer. And coming on the heels of World War I, beer, with its German connotation, was singled out for being particularly unpatriotic. Carrie Nation, a temperance movement leader, said of the city in 1902: "If there is any place that is hell on earth, it is Milwaukee."

Crime rose spectacularly across the nation in the first half of the 1920s, more than 33 percent according to a report out of the attorney general's office. It was estimated that half of the increase in the crime rate had to do with alcohol-related offenses. The effect of prohibition, and man's keen desire to have his drink whether it be legal or not, also contributed to a steep rise in civil cases. The number of illegal booze joints skyrocketed; in Milwaukee, they were often called "blind pigs."

Fortunately, organized crime didn't have the stranglehold on Milwaukee during the Prohibition era that it did with the city's bigger neighbor to the south. Chicago featured probably the era's most famous mobster, Al Capone, and had one of the highest murder rates in the country in the 1920s.

It was said that many Chicago mobsters enjoyed vacationing in the woods along Lake Michigan north of Milwaukee and in other places in Wisconsin where they could escape the heat. However, Jacob Laubenheimer, Milwaukee's chief of police, introduced high-powered rifles, machine guns and even some armored squad cars to discourage Chicago gangsters. Laubenheimer refused to tolerate any "disruptive characters" in the city, with the result being that the slogan of the underworld became "Stay away from Milwaukee," according to the City of Milwaukee website.

While Wauwatosa started the decade as more of an isolated town, with much farmland surrounding the city, and with Milwaukee still at arm's length, it wasn't long before that solitude began to change. During the 1920s, Wauwatosa transitioned from a small town with horses and buggies to a major suburban area centered on the automobile. The decade started with 5,800 residents in town; the population had rocketed up to nearly 25,000 by 1930, growth overseen by A.C. Hanson, who served as mayor from 1920 to 1934. Milwaukee was also expanding to the west, toward Wauwatosa, and better roads and transportation brought the big city even closer.

A large German immigration wave in the 1890s brought "a sturdy folk with high notions of justice and integrity to Wauwatosa," according to *The Story of Wauwatosa*, published in 1935. People were drawn to the city by its "beautiful natural topography, the pure artesian water, high caliber of residents and the excellent schools."

The start of the 1920s brought a better street lighting system, the establishment of a park board and the purchase of nineteen acres just across State Street from John Armstrong's business for City Park, now Hart Park.

The house in which Buddy Schumacher lived in 1925 was near State Street, the main east–west thoroughfare from Milwaukee to the Village. A

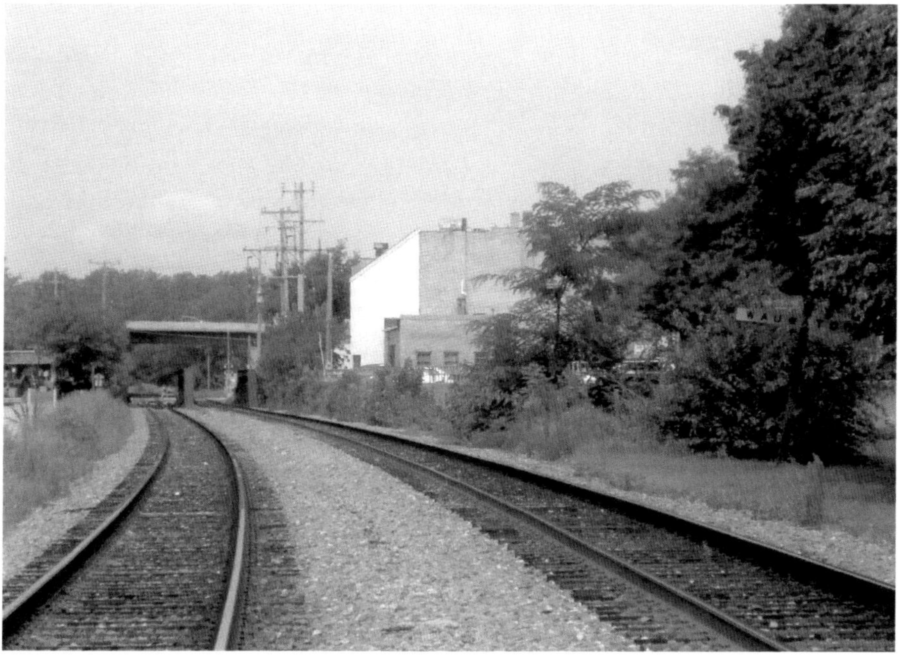

The railroad tracks, looking west, near where the Wauwatosa depot used to stand, across State Street from the Schumacher house.

local newspaper story in 1915 boasted that State Street gave Wauwatosa "one of the best and longest asphalt roads in the county."

The Minneapolis and St. Paul Railroad and the Menomonee River also cut east–west through this area of Wauwatosa, both paralleling State Street until they hit Harwood Avenue, at which point the river and tracks both curve to the northwest. Easy access to the area from Milwaukee sometimes brought vagrants, some of whom set up camps in the "yunkles" (a German term for "jungles") along the Menomonee River just west of town, near Blackridge. The vagrant issue was a relatively new one for Wauwatosa. In 1912, in fact, Police Chief George Baltes had actually begged the city's only tramp to stay, according to a *Milwaukee Journal* story.

One of the major economic forces in Wauwatosa then, as it is today, was healthcare. In the middle of the nineteenth century, Milwaukee County purchased land on the west side of Wauwatosa for the county hospital, which housed the poor, sick and insane all within one farmhouse. The Muirdale Sanitorium was opened in 1915 on the Milwaukee County Institution Grounds west of the Village. This facility was mainly a treatment center for tuberculosis sufferers. The Milwaukee Psychiatric Hospital, originally named the Milwaukee Sanitorium, was also just west of the Village and was used for the treatment of nervous disorders.

Insanity was an increasingly popular topic in the area in the 1920s. A story in the *Milwaukee Sentinel* in May 1926 cited William L. Coffey, manager of the Milwaukee County institutions, as stating that "insanity in Milwaukee County is on the increase," noting a steady rise since the start of prohibition.

The editorial noted that the hospital for mental diseases in Wauwatosa was "crowded to the doors" and that sixty patients had been farmed out to other facilities in Wisconsin. The city's asylum for the chronically insane was also crowded. The county facilities for such treatment were also housing more patients than ever before.

So, while Wauwatosa in the 1920s was known for its beauty, safety, great schools and beautiful scenery, it was not totally without danger. Wauwatosa's parents most certainly warned their children to watch where they went.

It seemed that Buddy Schumacher may not have heeded all the warnings.

Chapter 5

BUDDY DISAPPEARS

It was a comfortable summer morning Buddy Schumacher awoke to on Friday, July 24, 1925. The sun was out, the temperature was rising past the seventy-degree mark on the way to a high of about seventy-five that day. After breakfast, at about 9:00 a.m., the brown-haired, blue-eyed boy with an engaging smile waved goodbye to his sister and went to meet up with some friends. He never came back alive.

The first few newspaper reports after Buddy disappeared that day noted that he was with Arnold Yunk and Jack Wolf, both ten-year-olds who lived near him and attended school with him. But after a few days, the newspaper stories consistently reported that Buddy was with Yunk, ten, who lived one house north of the Schumachers, at 197 Alice Street, and brothers John and Gordon Wolf, twelve and ten respectively, who lived around the corner at 72 State Street, present site of a bar named Colonel Hart's.

Considering how much conflicting information and errors were contained in the newspaper reports during this investigation, it would not come as a shock to find out that an error was made in reporting how many boys were with Buddy at the time of his disappearance. It's odd, though, that John "Jack" Wolf was said to be ten years old in the first few articles but his age was corrected to twelve later on.

There seems to be a consensus among multiple newspaper reports concerning at least a few facts surrounding Buddy's disappearance. Buddy and his friends decided to head toward the local swimming hole, an island called Blackridge in the Menomonee River just south of the site of the present Tosa Pool at Hoyt Park, about a mile northwest of the Village.

In the 1920s and 1930s, community members swam in this earth-bottom swimming hole filled each summer by the Wauwatosa Fire Department, according to the Friends of Hoyt Park and Pool website. In 1939, a public pool was built on this site with part of the river filled in so that there is no longer an island there.

Instead of walking to the swimming hole, the boys figured they'd jump on, or "hook," one of the freight trains that routinely headed west from the Wauwatosa train depot, situated directly across State Street from the Schumacher home. Sometime after disembarking from the train, Buddy went with an unknown man, while the rest of the boys went home.

How and where this man appeared and how the boys reacted to him is in question, as the boys' stories changed a few times. A story in the *Milwaukee Journal* the evening of the disappearance noted that Jack Wolf and Arnold Yunk (his Americanized name was Jung) told Buddy's mother that they had all been chased away from the swimming hole by someone but "couldn't explain what happened to Arthur."

The *Milwaukee Sentinel* reported the next morning that Jack Wolf and Arnold Yunk were with Buddy when he disappeared. The boys said that they were too frightened at first to tell anyone what happened, causing the delay in discussing it. They said that they were at the swimming hole when "an unkempt, unshaven man" showed up and chased them into the woods, where they became separated from one another. Yunk and Wolf said that they never saw Buddy or this man again.

However, in a page-one *Milwaukee Journal* story later that day, Jack Wolf and Arnold Yunk told Wauwatosa police that they were with Buddy "at the stone quarry when the man appeared suddenly from the bushes and threatened them." Wolf told police that he and Yunk ran in one direction and Buddy ran in another when the man appeared. The boys said that the man, described as tall and poorly dressed, seemed to be gaining on Buddy along the right-of-way on the Milwaukee Road tracks when they lost sight of him.

The July 27 newspapers were the first to report that both Wolf brothers were with Buddy when he went missing three days earlier. The boys had been questioned for several hours, according to a story in the *Milwaukee Sentinel*, and "they stuck to their story solidly" that they were chased by a "tough looking" young man on the railroad tracks.

At one point, John Wolf gave the following account of what happened to a *Milwaukee Sentinel* reporter:

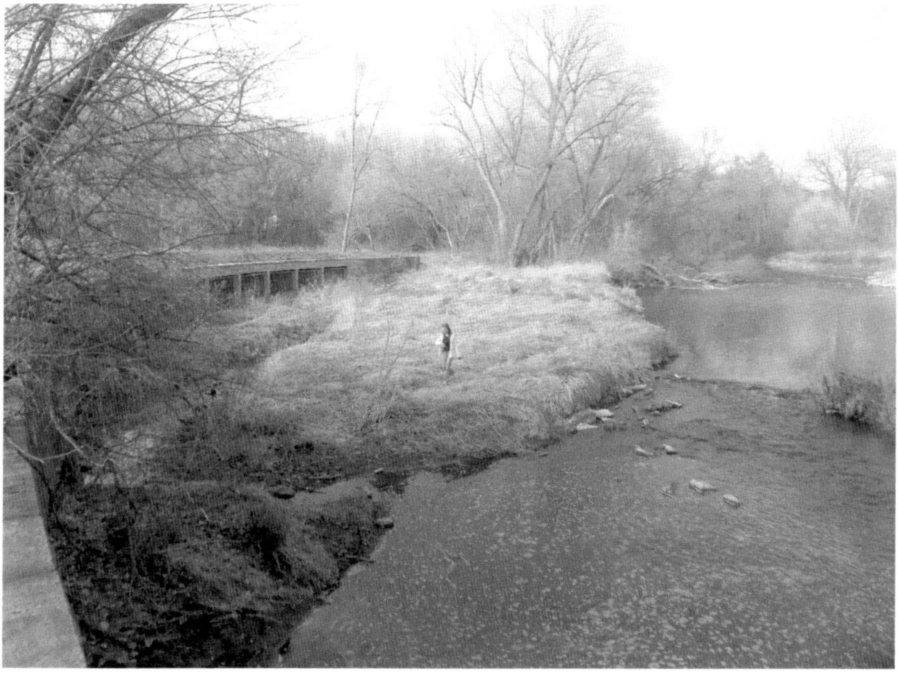

This is the area where Buddy Schumacher and his friends were heading when he disappeared. The city fire department used to flood this area of the Menomonee River, called Blackridge, each summer, and it served as a swimming hole a little northwest of the Village in Wauwatosa.

> *We were going to Blackridge, hooked the train while it was going slow. Out this side of the swimmin' hole we thought that the train was speeding up and we had better hop off. Just when we were getting ready to jump a fellow up on one of the cars hollered at us.*
>
> *He said to me "Where are them kids going?"*
>
> *I didn't say anything, but we jumped off. Then he jumped off and chased us. We ran across the creek, jumping on stones sticking out of the water. Arnold was ahead, Gordon next and I was last. Arthur stood on the tracks and didn't run.*
>
> *Well this man chased us to Kenyon Avenue and then he went back to where Arthur was. We didn't want to go back and we thought Arthur could get home alone all right.*

Police, however, weren't so sure this was really what happened. "The authorities are inclined to discredit the story and further efforts to quiz the

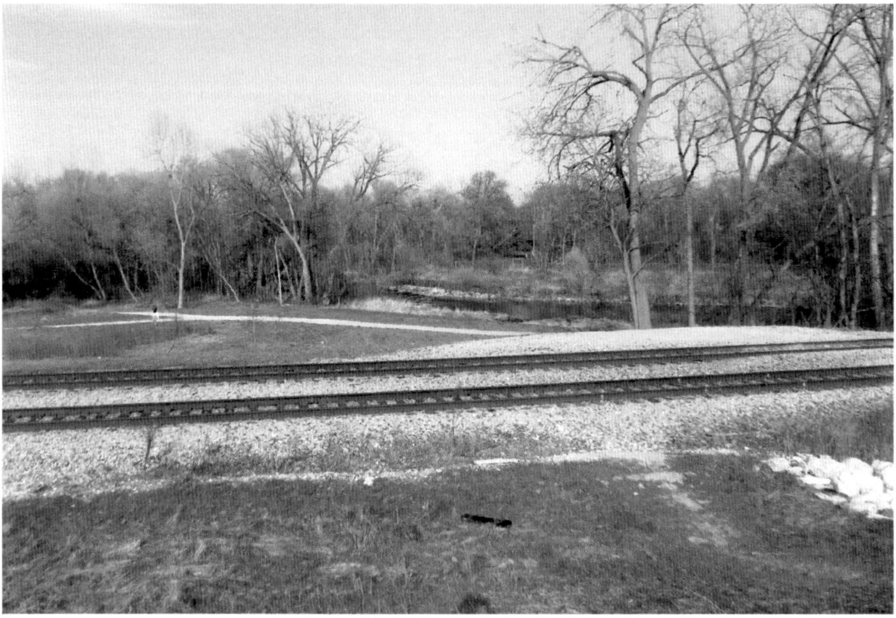

A view of the former swimming hole from above the railroad tracks that pass nearby. It is said that Buddy Schumacher and some friends had jumped aboard a freight train heading toward the swimming hole but were scared from the train by a mysterious man before it got there.

boys will be made," according to a *Milwaukee Journal* report. By this time, the district attorney, Eugene Wengert, had assigned Detective Adolph Kraemer and Deputy Sheriff John M. Mahoney to the case. When the *Milwaukee Sentinel* came out on Tuesday morning, July 28, it noted that the previous day, Kraemer and Mahoney had taken Arnold Yunk back to the spot where he said Buddy disappeared.

The boy retold the story, although this time he said that the boys had been "accosted by the man in a blue suit who rode the train." After being chased from the train, the boys ran until they escaped into the woods. Buddy didn't run, Yunk told police this time, and when the man gave up chasing his companions, he returned to Buddy. The *Milwaukee Journal*'s July 28 story, "Degenerates Hunted in Search for Child," also noted that the boys' story had changed. They said in this story that they were not chased and that Buddy walked down the track after the man.

A Milwaukee Road trackman, meanwhile, gave yet another account of the incident. Charles Polko said he was on the right-of-way west of the city about a quarter mile from the swimming hole when a westbound train passed him, according to stories in both the *Journal* and *Sentinel* on July 27.

He said he saw a man fitting the general description given by the boys run out to the train and hop on. At the swimming hole, three boys got off the train, according to Polko. But he did not see the man get off. Polko said that he didn't pay much attention to the boys, so he wouldn't be able to recognize them. But he did say that a fourth boy, clad in overalls, remained on a boxcar.

This statement seemed to lend support to the theory that Buddy had been carried off by a train. However, that couldn't be substantiated "after sixty hours of inquiry in which railroad officials have cooperated whole heartedly," according to the *Sentinel* of July 27.

The railroad employee named as Charles Polko that day in the papers apparently had a new name just a few days later. The *Journal* and *Sentinel* both reported in their August 2 editions that a Milwaukee Road section hand by the name of Frank Blue had spurred authorities into focusing their investigation on the railroad's right-of-way with his contradiction of the three companions' story.

"I was working on the tracks and saw the strange man described by the boys as he ran for the freight," Blue was quoted in an August 2 *Sentinel* article.

> *I saw the three youngsters jump from the train, but the fourth one, apparently the Schumacher boy, didn't get off and when the train went around the curve he was hanging on to the brake wheel, almost flat on his stomach on top of a box car.*
>
> *The man didn't get off either and I saw him sitting on a car as the train went out of sight. He was about three cars ahead of the caboose and the boy was on a car about the middle of the train.*

Blue said that the freight train picked up speed as it passed through the yards, and he decided that in spite of all his railroad experience, he would not have jumped off or onto the moving freight. "I thought the little fellow was scared to death by the way he was lying on top of the car," he added. "It's beyond me to understand how he could get off that train after it hit the downgrade into Elm Grove and Brookfield, where they clip along at forty miles an hour."

So was the man who gave this story Charles Polko or Frank Blue? Did the newspapers both interview this man, and did both get his name wrong the first time? From the stories, it didn't sound like the papers talked to two different railroad men. Since later references call this man Frank Blue, we'll stick with that and assume that Blue and Polko are one in the same.

By the time the *Wauwatosa News* was finally able to publish information on the case, it had been nearly a week since the boy had vanished. The local newspaper reported that according to Buddy's pals, all four boys hopped on the train in the city and then were chased off the train by "a vagabond," who ran after them. When they escaped, he then returned to Buddy, who apparently did not run away. This version became the accepted story in further coverage.

Exactly how Buddy was accosted isn't known; all we have are some educated guesses. First of all, how reliable were Buddy's pals? At first, there were two of them, then there were three. They changed their stories. Is it possible that these were the same boys who tied Buddy to a tree while playing "Indian" "in the Wauwatosa Yunkles," once causing him to come home several hours after dinnertime? If so, could they have been trying to pull another prank on him? Is it possible that these older boys took advantage of their young friend's naïveté, thinking that it may be fun to run away from him, and then the ruse went unintentionally tragic? The boys were described as "good friends and often played together" in a *Wauwatosa News* story on September 17. However, this may have been one way that the *News* tried to protect Yunk and the Wolf brothers.

There seems to be enough evidence to support the theory that a vagrant did surprise the boys at some point, whether it was on the train or off the train. The man and Buddy may have stayed on the train on down the line a bit, or the man may have chased after the boys after they jumped from the train.

Buddy may still have been naïve about the kind of men who rode the rails back then. Many were out of work and/or mentally ill, and at the age of eight, Buddy may not have fully grasped what kinds of dangers meeting up with one could mean, especially if he was surprised by one on the train. It's possible that Buddy's older companions, no matter the number of them, were more keenly aware of the potential danger of such situations. And when faced with this one, they ran, forgetting that Buddy might need a reminder.

It would seem that Buddy's pals would have been quite rattled by this experience, too. To have their friend kidnapped must have been traumatic—especially a younger one they most likely either felt obligated to watch over or may have been expected to watch over. They may have very well felt that Buddy's disappearance was their fault. They ran; Buddy did not. Why didn't they grab him?

It seems that the boys simply went home, hoping that everything would be all right. It wasn't.

Chapter 6

THE SEARCH BEGINS

When Buddy didn't come home that night, Art Schumacher started asking around. Among the first people he went to see were Yunk and the Wolf boys. As it got late, and their boy still had not returned home, Art and Florence held out the faint hope that their son had spent the night at a relative's house, even though the youngster had never been away from home overnight by himself before.

When Buddy didn't show up the next morning, his mother and father frantically organized a posse to search the area where his companions had said they last saw him. They immediately enlisted friends and neighbors to scour the area around the swimming hole, the railroad right-of-way, the Menomonee River and other nearby areas.

They were looking for a boy described as being four feet, eight inches tall and weighing sixty-five pounds, with good teeth and a tan complexion, in an August 15 edition of the *Waukesha Freeman*. He was said to have been wearing blue denim coveralls and canvas shoes when he was last seen.

Many areas surrounding the Menomonee River were overrun by tall weeds, some as tall as six feet. These areas were referred to at times as yunkles or jungles, and it was very difficult to see much through the dense foliage. But local residents were determined to push their way through these jungles in an effort to find the boy.

As the *Sentinel*'s story of July 26 reported, "Led by the indefatigable mother and the equally tireless father, the searching party, which grew in size as the alarm spread throughout the neighborhood, was methodically scouring the wide expanse of wasteland and 'Yunkles.'" As the sky darkened, searchers brought out lanterns "which flashed like will o' wisps through the swamps and thickets as the hunt went on." Even at midnight, more than fifty citizens—both men and women—were still voluntarily searching in wells, under the foundations of buildings and in ravines, wooded areas and the swamps along the river.

Wauwatosa police and firemen met with concerned citizens at 8:00 p.m. the night after the disappearance before separating into small groups, each taking a different direction in a cross-country search of the ravines and woods near where Buddy disappeared. The search extended several miles.

All the Wauwatosa police were called in by Chief George Baltes, and the officers were instructed to arrest anyone "who could not give a satisfactory account of himself," a *Journal* story noted. After just one day of searching, Baltes surmised that Buddy "is either a prisoner of the man who chased him or he is the victim of a tragedy."

Baltes left for the west-central Wisconsin city of La Crosse later that night to bring back a man arrested there by a railroad detective earlier in the day. A description of the man sent via telegraph matched up well with the description given by Yunk and one of the Wolf brothers. The plan was for the boys to try to identify the man when Baltes returned with him the next day. In this story, the *Sentinel* reported that "the two survivors" will attempt to identify the man, inferring that Buddy had already perished.

News of Buddy's disappearance hit the radio waves that day, too. Radio was in its infancy at the time as the first broadcasting license in the United States had just been granted four years earlier, and only 5 million of the country's homes had radio receivers, as they were called then. That equates to roughly one-fifth of the homes in America. So, although radio was booming at this time, use of this medium to spread news was still rather unique.

The *Milwaukee Journal*/Marquette University radio station WHAD (273 on the dial in those days), as well as WSOE of the Milwaukee School of Engineering (246), broadcast the boy's description on Saturday afternoon at the request of Buddy's mother. Milwaukee police were also given orders to be on the lookout for the boy.

By the end of the first day of the search, Florence Schumacher was so overcome with exhaustion and worry over her son's absence that she was in the care of a physician at home. Although haggard from lack of sleep, Art Schumacher pressed on. Dejected and discouraged, he still tried to rally the groups of friends that had come to his aid.

The death of famed attorney William Jennings Bryan dominated page one of the Monday morning, July 27 *Milwaukee Sentinel*. But even as Bryan's

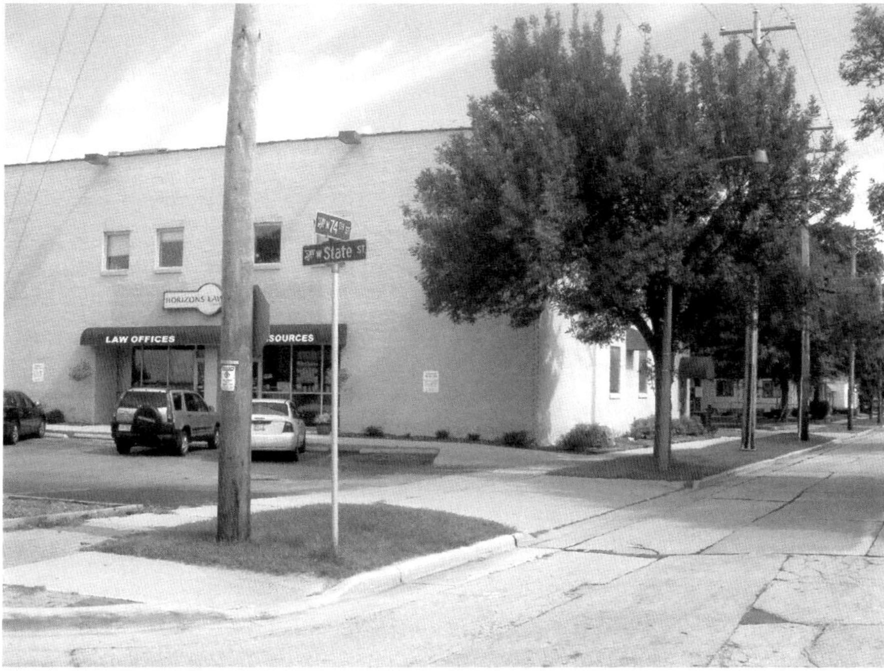

The corner of Seventy-fourth and State Streets in Wauwatosa. Buddy Schumacher's grandfather, John Armstrong, once had a horseshoeing business here, when it was the corner of Alice Street and Watertown Plank Road. In 1925, the Schumacher family lived one property north of this corner at 191 Alice Street. The property is now a parking lot.

death was big news that day, so was Buddy Schumacher. In fact, this headline was stretched across the very top of the paper, above the *Milwaukee Sentinel* masthead: "60-Hour Search for Missing Boy Proves Fruitless."

On Sunday, the second day of the search for Buddy Schumacher, two hundred searchers failed to come up with any clues after looking in all the rural areas adjacent to Wauwatosa. By then, railroad companies, as well as citizens and police in many southern Wisconsin towns, had become involved.

The first person of interest in the case was cleared when Baltes returned from La Crosse, saying that the man under arrest there proved that he was in St. Paul, Minnesota, when Buddy vanished. Soon, a vagrant in Wauwatosa was questioned about the Schumacher case. Edward Vreeland was taken into custody by Wauwatosa police officers Louis Wrasse and Ernst Hammerschmidt on the farm of William Fisher, a mile west of the city, for harassing boys. Fisher had noticed Vreeland living not far from his farmhouse on a creek for six weeks. Fisher said that while he did not like the man's appearance, he didn't object to his presence. Two days after the boy disappeared, Fisher said that he had started into some nearby woods on the farm of C.A. Koepfler. As he passed by Vreeland's camp, Fisher said that Vreeland engaged him in conversation.

"It was the first time the man had spoken to me and I was surprised," Fisher said. "I thought at the time that for some reason he did not want me to go up into the woods. He kept walking along beside me, talking all the time and directing my attention to the creek and railroad. As I continued up to the woods, I saw he watched me constantly. I became suspicious of him then and called police."

Arnold Yunk, one of Buddy's pals, was brought in to see Vreeland and said that he'd never seen him before. Vreeland was determined not to be the mysterious man who was last seen with Buddy Schumacher, but this would not be the only time Vreeland was linked to this story.

By the time Buddy had been missing for forty-eight hours, hundreds were searching the area, and bloodhounds had traced his trail to the edge of the river. There, the animals stopped in confusion, and none was able to tell whether the trail ended at the railroad track or the river.

Some feared that he had drowned. But if he had drowned, officials figured that it would have been just a matter of a few hours before the body would float to the surface. Some thought that he might have been carried away on the train. But most figured that he had met some terrible fate at the hands of a vagrant. But without any concrete evidence, no theory could be dismissed. So, as any unusual sightings of a young boy continued to be reported, city or county officials checked them out.

Just a few days after Buddy disappeared, District Attorney Wengert was informed that Art Schumacher had been threatened "several years ago" by a man who said that he would seek revenge on Art for something Art had done to him. In one of the newspaper reports, this man was said to be a relative of Art's. The identity of this man was never revealed, although reports did say that he was questioned and that authorities believed he had no connection to Buddy's disappearance.

Just about this time, Wengert assigned two of Milwaukee County's best detectives to the case: Adolph Kraemer and Bruno Zellmer, both of whom would go on to long and distinguished careers on the Milwaukee police force and who were often teamed together on difficult cases.

Kraemer, who was forty-six years old when the crime was committed, finished his career as Milwaukee's chief of detectives, retiring in 1954 after a forty-nine-year career with the force. He'd been on the force nearly twenty-one years when Buddy went missing. In a *Milwaukee Sentinel* story announcing his retirement, it was noted that Kramer had taken part in many famous criminal investigations, including two infamous murders in recent years. One involved the disappearance of Cecelia Lemay and her stepson, Homer Lemay, which necessitated a trip to Argentina. That case was never solved. Kraemer was successful in the other case mentioned, finding the killer of a fifteen-year-old girl.

Kraemer received public praise from Milwaukee police chief John Polcyn upon Kramer's retirement, including mention that Kraemer excelled in the area of criminal psychology.

Less is known about Zellmer, although he was part of quite a law enforcement family. He started in 1900, so he'd already put twenty-five years on the job by the Schumacher case. He retired in 1931, about two months after being assigned to night duty as he was going through a divorce. Zellmer's grandson, Orval A. Zellmer, spent thirty-five years in the Milwaukee Police Department, retiring as assistant police chief, and another grandson, Douglas G. Zellmer, was a bodyguard for the Milwaukee mayor for a time. Robert Zellmer, a cousin of Orval and Douglas, was a police officer, too.

Wengert, a resident of Wauwatosa who had just been elected district attorney the year before at the age of thirty-nine, fashioned a reputation as a man of great integrity from his early days as a lawyer, then in the district attorney's office and eventually as a high-ranking official in the Northern District of the Lutheran Church's Missouri Synod. Wengert served as a judge in the Missouri Synod's highest religious court until a year before his death and was also a leader in conservationist organizations and as a representative to German and Austrian consuls in the area.

During his eight years in the district attorney's office, four as assistant DA, Wengert prosecuted unlicensed brokerage houses, began a campaign to put loan sharks out of business in Milwaukee County, was responsible for legislation making it easier for small firms to make loans, was a proponent of seeking pardons for prisoners "to remake them and fit them for society," criticized judges who sentenced prisoners "according to their mood or prejudice" and opposed laws proposed to ban the sale of alcohol on Sundays, saying that church and state should be separate.

Wengert was lauded at a dinner in December 1928 honoring him for his service as district attorney after his retirement from the post. Due to his deep religious convictions, it was said that Wengert was interested in the rights of man over the rights of property and money. It was said that he retired with a reputation that was "spotless and stainless."

While Wengert and the two detectives who did the most work on the case seemed to have had positive reputations, it's not as clear what kind of man the Wauwatosa chief of police was back in those days. George Baltes was appointed city marshal of Wauwatosa in 1909 and became chief when the police department was created. At the time of Buddy Schumacher's murder, Baltes was about forty-six years old. He resigned in 1932 after trying to cover up a shooting of one of his officers. The officer was intoxicated when he attempted to enter a closed grocery store in town and was shot by the store owner. The Wauwatosa Police Department website notes that Baltes was involved in the coverup with a sergeant and two officers.

What is not totally clear is if Baltes resigned because of this incident or because he caught wind that the city's police and fire commission were contemplating reducing police salaries, which would have negatively affected his pension.

The *Milwaukee Sentinel* and *Journal* reported that Baltes resigned because of the coverup; the *Wauwatosa News* noted that "it is mere co-incidence that it is tendered at this time" and, in an editorial, blasted the Milwaukee papers for its "smashing attack on Wauwatosa's police force, the police and fire commission" and pretty much everyone involved in the incident. "The action of the Milwaukee press is an incident; the Wauwatosa police force is an institution," the editorial trumpeted. The editorial referenced the Milwaukee reports as "characteristic of Mr. [William Randolph] Hearst and his minions. Their slogan is 'GORE IS MIGHTY AND SHALL PREVAIL.'"

It's unclear if the coverup was a common method in Baltes's repertoire or if it was viewed more as a one-time flub that was serious enough to warrant a forced resignation. And even if it was true that Baltes had a habit of underhanded tricks, would this have affected the way the Schumacher case was handled?

Baltes, Kraemer and Zellmer were the main men charged with finding Buddy and bringing his killer to justice. They chased every lead they had, although there were not many credible ones in the first days of the investigation. By the end of the day Monday after Buddy vanished, the search of the woods, fields and buildings in the area west of Wauwatosa where the lad was last seen had basically been abandoned.

Chapter 7

"WE'LL NEVER GIVE UP"

By the time the search for Buddy had reached seventy-two hours, most of the local speculation on his assumed kidnapper centered on homeless men who inhabited areas outside the city of Wauwatosa. Some men had set up camp near wooded areas or along the Menomonee River, and police had received some reports of these men harassing area youth from time to time.

One of the first such reports came on the Monday after Buddy disappeared. A Wauwatosa resident who lived a little south of the river, about half a mile from the Schumachers, told police that his son reported seeing a "degenerate" loitering in the woods near where Buddy had vanished. The boy said that the man had been persuading small boys to go into the woods with him by deceiving or flattering them and then sexually mistreating them. The July 28 *Milwaukee Journal* reported that two different men, who hung about nearby swimming holes, had tried to entice several local boys into the woods. These men apparently were working separately.

Late Monday, ten-year-old Lawrence Nelson, who lived at the Lutheran Children's Home, led searchers to "a yunkle of tall weeds and tangled underbrush surrounding the river," according to a *Wauwatosa News* story. Here, they found a well-hidden but deserted camp. Further questioning led investigators to determine that two men had camped here from April until the day Buddy disappeared. The men, who had been frequently seen in the company of young boys from the neighborhood, had not been seen since. Police believed that this was among the most important discoveries since the beginning of the search.

The *Milwaukee Sentinel* reported in its July 29 editions that this camp was at the end of a carefully hidden trail through the yunkles west of the Milwaukee Road tracks. Nelson said that these two middle-aged and unfriendly men who had been living here had frequently annoyed him and his friends, often chasing them. It was pointed out that one of these men might have easily made off with Buddy due to his familiarity with "the various parks and refuges of his yunkle home."

The Nelson boy took investigators into the area to show them the ruins of a hut that he and four companions from the children's home had built. The hut was under the overhanging edge of a bluff separated from the railroad tracks by about an eighth of a mile of tall weeds. "They tore the roof off our house," the boy said. "Two men who live over by that big tree," he added as he pointed to a tree in the densest part of the yunkle.

"They used to break into our hut and sleep here," Nelson continued. "Then we put a lock on it, and they tore off the roof and kicked it down. All the boys were afraid of them, and we run whenever they call us."

Several weeks before, the boys reported the men to Reverend Frank Wirts, superintendent of the children's home. Nelson said that the last time he'd seen the men was the day Buddy disappeared.

The boy led searchers to the big tree he'd pointed out by way of a well-worn path through the thickets. There was plenty of evidence of recent habitation there. The tree was on a knoll of high ground, and under it was a bench that could have been used as a bed. A cache of food was found in a tin pail under the bench. There were several eggs, half a loaf of bread and some rolls. The food was wrapped in a newspaper dated July 21. The boy described the two men as of medium height and probably between forty and sixty years old. One of them had a mustache, he said.

A man of about forty-four years old, who sported a mustache, was expected to be arrested soon, according to the July 29 *Milwaukee Sentinel*. The man "may be able to solve the mysterious disappearance," the story noted. Even if the arrest didn't lead to the solving of the Schumacher case, Detective Kraemer said it was at least expected to put an end to the misconduct described by several small boys who said they'd received money from the man.

Also on that day, it was reported that police were led on a wild goose chase when they got word of a boy matching Buddy's description seen riding on an eastbound train at Oconomowoc, about twenty-five miles west of Wauwatosa. The train wasn't flagged until it got through Wauwatosa and to the Hawley Street station on the far west side of Milwaukee. The boy in question "made off" with a man, and both were captured after "an hour's chase." The boy turned out not to be Buddy, and the man turned out to be the boy's father. It was determined that they were both heading back home to Chicago.

On Tuesday morning, July 28, home subscribers picked up their *Milwaukee Sentinel* and saw "Fear Boy Is Moron's Prey" in large bold type screaming across the top of the front page. Customers who plunked their three cents down at the newsstand to purchase a copy of the Latest City Edition were treated to a similar headline: "Fear Moron Took Boy." This story included more reports from children of a man attempting to lure them into the woods near Wauwatosa, and several other boys told Police Chief Baltes of another "moron" who had been loitering about another swimming hole on the Menomonee River, this one just east of Wauwatosa at Fifty-ninth Street. The man was reported to entice boys into the woods by offering them money and then molesting them.

Police told the newspaper that there was a possibility that this man had learned of the swimming hole west of town and decided to try that area, too. The boys who told police about the man who frequented the Fifty-ninth Street swimming hole were asked to come into the police station to see two men who had been taken into custody. Neither, the boys said, was the man they had seen, and the men were released.

Still, an abduction by a homeless man seemed to be the most plausible explanation for what had happened to Buddy. Two other suppositions about Buddy's disappearance were all but abandoned before the first week of searching was up. The theory that he'd been carried off by the train to parts west and north of the city didn't seem to be going anywhere, although Milwaukee Road officials were still cooperating with Police Chief Baltes. It was said that no track worker, yardman or station agent on the entire system between Wauwatosa and La Crosse had found the slightest trace of the boy. Railroad employees continued to hunt but were confident that Buddy hadn't traveled on the train any farther than the swimming hole.

Also, the fear that the boy may have drowned was looking less likely as the river bottom had been thoroughly searched by divers and expert crews, and authorities found it impossible for a body to have escaped notice under such circumstances.

Five days after his son had gone missing, Art Schumacher was sounding like a man who was beginning to accept his worst fears. "Arthur is either dead or hundreds of miles away," he was quoted as telling reporters. "I feel that this vicinity has been so thoroughly searched, he would have been found were he nearby."

The *Wauwatosa News* shared Mr. Schumacher's sentiments. "The boy has vanished off the face of the earth," the story reported. "Despite the fact that the radio has flashed the notice of the lad's disappearance over the entire country, no news has been gained up to the present time. Where he is, where his body lies, if he has been killed, is one of the biggest mysteries of its kind in the neighborhood."

Nevertheless, the search continued and was even ramped up. At Detective Kraemer's request, assistant Boy Scout executive Harold C. Davies made an appeal through the newspapers and the radio asking Milwaukee-area Scouts to search for the boy. About fifty to sixty Scouts gathered at the Wauwatosa police station at 9:00 a.m. on July 30 to embark on a search throughout the Menomonee River Valley for the entire morning. The boys walked fifty abreast one yard apart while tramping down weeds and tearing apart thickets and clumps of underbrush. Their efforts, led by Davies and Wauwatosa scoutmaster Alfred Johnson, as well as Chief Baltes and Deputy Sheriff Frank Mahoney, proved fruitless. After returning to the station to eat lunches they'd brought with them, the Scouts went back out, searching even farther. No signs of the boy were found, convincing authorities that the boy was not in the river valley.

Even though authorities were sure by this time that Buddy hadn't drowned, the river was once again dragged by Captain T.F. Boutin, a man in his early sixties who was a former member of the Coast Guard and was well known for the recovery of drowned bodies and also in using the relatively new technique of artificial respiration to save lives of those who might have otherwise drowned. Boutin was credited with saving twenty-eight lives, the first of which came when he was seven years old. One of Boutin's earliest successes was when he saved his uncle who had fallen off a dock and had been hit on the head by a barrel of fish when he came to the surface. Boutin had no such luck finding Buddy, though. After working all day, Boutin was convinced that Buddy's body was not in the Menomonee River anywhere near the place he disappeared.

Meanwhile, Wauwatosa residents also pitched in financially to try and help find the boy. A $250 reward offered by the local business association was matched by Buddy's father for a total of $500 for information leading to his son's return. The business community's offer was announced by J.E. Robertson, owner of Robertson Hardware in downtown Wauwatosa and president of the Wauwatosa Commercial Association. That was augmented by neighbors with another $500, the latter amount to be paid to anyone who returned the boy alive or gave information by which the boy could be found alive. At first, Art would not accept the additional $500, but the offer was held open in case the situation warranted it.

The parents' hopes of finding their son alive faded with each passing day. A story in the July 31 *Milwaukee Sentinel* noted: "A flickering spark of hope—the kind of dogged, unreasoning hope which survives everything but actual proof of death—was all that was left last night between Mr. and Mrs.

Schumacher and despair." A photo of Florence Schumacher looking out the doorway of her home accompanied the story with the headline "WITH ACHING HEART, SHE AWAITS HER BOY" and the following text: "Hoping, praying, waiting, watching, and repeating over and over again 'Where is my boy? Where, where is he?' This woman is keeping sleepless vigil while her husband, assisted by scores of searchers, keeps on with the hunt for their 8 year old son, Arthur, missing since last Friday. She is Mrs. Arthur Schumacher, and she is shown as she appeared last night in the doorway of her home, peering through the darkness in a vain hope for her boy."

Art Schumacher, meanwhile, was described after coming home for the sixth straight night without his son: "A wan smile, a shake of the head, and mumbled words of encouragement meant to instill a confidence the speaker did not feel—these were all the sorely-tried father could bring home to the strangely silent cottage at 195 Alice Street." Even at this late date in the saga, the paper did not get the Schumachers' address correct.

"But we'll never give up," Florence Schumacher was quoted as saying. "We'll keep looking and looking until we find him." When she said this, Florence was feeling stronger than at any time since her collapse two days after her boy vanished. "I'll be out again in a day or so," she said, "and I'm going right back and keep on with the hunt. The boy is somewhere and I know I will never be able to rest easy until he is found or I know what happened to him." She ended up not being able to continue her searching for some time.

At some point, the reward was raised to $1,000 for information leading to the boy, whether dead or alive. News of the reward spread quickly, and local residents noted that almost all the searchers who toted lanterns late Saturday night August 1 looking through ground that had already been searched thoroughly numerous times had emerged from vehicles carrying out-of-state license plates.

Despite losing hope that he'd find his boy alive, Art Schumacher dedicated his life to finding his only son. In fact, about a week after his son had disappeared, it was reported that Art devised a plan to go into the hobo camps around the area and the state and disguise himself as one of them in order to gather clues to his son's fate and whereabouts. Since it was generally accepted that Buddy had been kidnapped by one of these vagrants, Art figured that the only way to find out what happened to his son was to mingle with them. A *Milwaukee Sentinel* story on August 1 told of Art Schumacher's plan with a huge page-one headline that read "BECOMES TRAMP TO FIND SON."

The night before, Art "consecrated the next few months of his life to an exhaustive search for his son throughout the state," the story reported. "He will

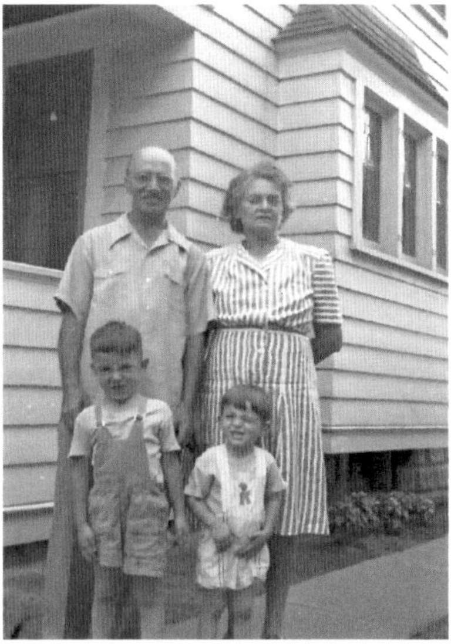

Art and Florence Schumacher at 8118 Hillcrest Drive with their grandsons, Brian and Gerald.

become a pilgrim, wandering at random, through highways and byways, seeking a clew which will solve the mystery which has aroused and puzzled the entire state." Art was to don the clothes of a hobo, "mingle with tramps in their refuges and yunkles, eating with them, sleeping with them, and above all, talking to them." He planned to hang out at railroad depots, tourist camps and any place homeless wanderers of the highways and rails may gather.

His planned search was further characterized like this: "Pursuing his quest with the fortitude of a knight of old, he will keep his eyes and ears open night and day for a word of cheer to send home to his waiting wife—the bereaved mother of the missing boy." It was in order to comfort his dear Florence that Art dreamed up the plan, the story noted, quoting him as telling his wife:

> *The boy is somewhere, and the fact that our searching has failed to find his body is almost conclusive proof that he is alive.*
>
> *These men who live along the railroad tracks in yunkle refuges such as we have found near here are the ones who will probably know more about where he is than any one else. I will become one of them, win their confidence, and will share their secrets.*
>
> *If I keep on long enough, somehow, somewhere I am going to get word of the boy. Somebody, in some way, will let slip a word which will put me on the right track. Then I will find him and bring him home to you.*

Her husband's announcement put a smile on Florence's face for the first time in days, according the newspaper account, "and her eyes there blazed anew the hope which anxious days of futile searching had almost extinguished."

Art was to begin this quest in a few days, delaying the start of it only long enough to make sure that he was no longer of any service in the search in Wauwatosa. Clad in ragged overalls, Art planned to start on foot down the railroad, described in the story as "a modern Jason, en route on one of the most unique missions ever devised."

Chapter 8

LEADS ALL OVER THE STATE

Art Schumacher never did dress as a hobo and become one of them. The same day that the morning *Sentinel* announced these plans it said Art had made, the afternoon's *Journal* contradicted them. While Art did state that he would never give up the search for his son and that he thought Buddy was still alive, the *Journal* reported that Art "denied that he would ride freight trains and visit hobo camps through the country to try to find his son."

Certainly, however, Buddy's case was shedding light on other missing child cases in the area. The *Sentinel*'s August 1 story on the Schumacher case concluded with updates on two other missing children: a seven-year-old boy who returned to his Milwaukee home after having walked to Racine to visit an uncle; and no further traces found of a seven-year-old Chicago boy who, it had been feared, may have run away with the circus. The *Sentinel*'s coverage that day also included a photo of Buddy's sister, Jeannette, holding her brother's slingshot. "It was only a week ago he was playing with this," the caption quoted eleven-year-old Jeanette as saying.

Meanwhile, Detective Kramer told the *Milwaukee Sentinel* that he also thought the boy was alive and still in Wisconsin. At the end of this story appeared a short story on two teenage brothers from West Allis who had been reported missing by their mother. They'd last been seen three days before Buddy disappeared. Two days later, the developments in the Schumacher case as reported by the *Milwaukee Sentinel* were once again followed by news of missing children, this time a small report on five boys who had gotten "the carnival bug" and followed a show from Milwaukee to Kenosha before being picked up by police and returned home.

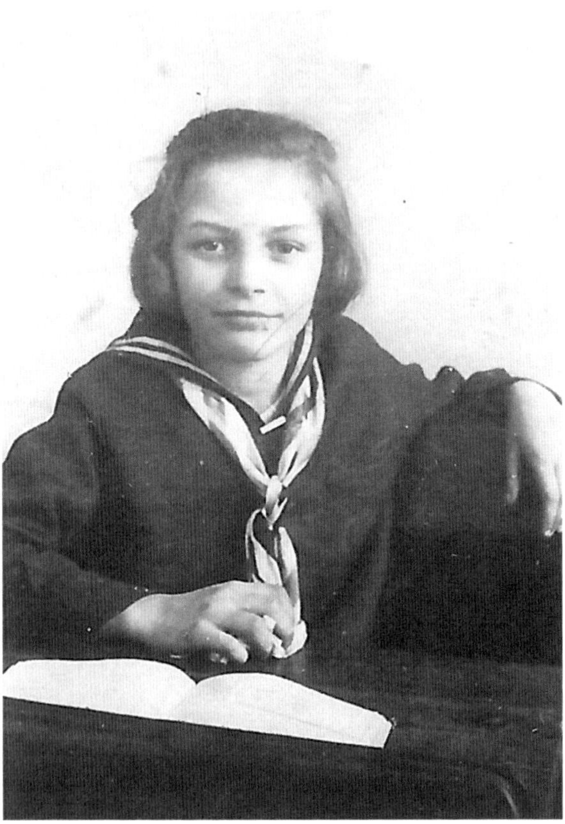

Jeanette Schumacher, 1923.

Within a little more than a week of Buddy vanishing, three hundred Milwaukee County deputies were on the case under the direction of Milwaukee County undersheriff Herman "Sonny" Kroening. The deputies were never able to find any clues to Buddy's whereabouts. Dynamiting of the Wauwatosa Quarry, a location presently occupied by a grocery store at Sixty-eighth and State Streets, did not reveal any clues either.

Chief Baltes sent letters to more than one hundred cities asking police to be on the lookout, and every railroad station along the Milwaukee Road was notified to repeat a thorough search of its area. Soon, some anonymous letters of a threatening nature began to appear at the sheriff's office. One of these letters was addressed to Milwaukee County sheriff Charles Reichenbach. It was postmarked in Stevens Point, in the central part of the state, and was written in ink in what was described as a masculine handwriting. Some of the note was undecipherable. Only two lines were legible: "Better qit looking for merders. They do not exist!"

The Schumacher case began to evoke memories in the area of the disappearance of young Charley Ross of Germantown, Pennsylvania, more than fifty years earlier as the Wauwatosa paper and at least one Milwaukee paper included stories of Charley's 1874 disappearance. Charley was kidnapped from the side of his brother and never heard from again. Abductors offered to return the boy for a $20,000 ransom but failed to appear at the designated rendezvous. Thirty-two years later, two robbers who were shot while resisting capture confessed to the abduction. However, they refused to reveal what they'd done to the youth or where they hid the body. In Wauwatosa, fifty-one years later, residents still held out a bit of hope that Buddy had not met a similar fate.

By the end of July, reports were starting to come in every day or so from various places in Wisconsin of a boy fitting Buddy's description. Reports came in from Columbus and Portage of a young couple with a crying boy fitting Buddy's description who was heard yelling at them that they were not his parents and pleading not to be hit again. Several witnesses reported seeing a boy about eight years old or so with this couple, and three identified the boy as Buddy Schumacher from a photo of Buddy. The lead was so strong that Detective Kraemer felt certain "he is on a warm trail," according to a story in the July 31 *Milwaukee Journal*.

Mrs. Josephine Reals, the proprietor of a café in Columbus, first reported the couple and the boy the Sunday after he disappeared. Kraemer also met with Robert Schultz of the Globe Hotel in Portage who said he'd seen the three in question, too.

According to the *Journal* story, Schultz said that the couple was in the hotel that day asking about various highways. Schultz said he could tell that the boy had been crying and then broke into tears again, wailing to the woman, "I want my mamma. You're not my mamma." When the man motioned to the boy to be quiet, the boy cried out, "Don't you slap me anymore; you're not my papa!" Reals said that the scene in her restaurant earlier that day was similar.

The woman who was said to be with the boy was described as about thirty-three years old with brown, bobbed hair, a dark suit and an orange hat. There was no description given of the man with whom she was traveling. The party was said to be driving in a Ford sedan with a Sheboygan license plate number. Authorities in those areas were warned to be on the lookout.

Police traced the license plate to a home in Sheboygan. A man answered the phone when Wauwatosa police called the house, but the man denied having been out of Sheboygan for the past two days. Detective Kramer then took Josephine Reals and her husband to Sheboygan to see if she could identify the man. She could not, and Kramer said that Columbus residents must have made a mistake in license plate numbers.

The very same day of the Columbus and Portage reports, a boy thought to match Buddy's description was seen in the company of two men in West Wrightstown, now part of Wrightstown between Appleton and Green Bay. Wrightstown postmaster Urban B. Remmel said that two vagrants called at a little house near the railroad asking how far it was to Appleton, according to a story in the *Appleton Post-Crescent*. A young woman, Mrs. Sherman LeRoy, answered the door and reportedly chastised the men. "Aren't you big fellows ashamed of yourselves, bumming rides with a young chap like that?" The boy reportedly replied, "I ain't cold." The three asked where Highway 15 was and started to walk in the direction of Appleton.

Wauwatosa police chief Baltes, who had seen every other lead dry up thus far, said that if this Wrightstown lead didn't pan out, there would be nothing else to work on. "We're up against a stone wall," he said.

Appleton city marshal George T. Prim, in the middle of an almost fifty-year career in police work that included twenty-five years in the Chicago Police Department before his move to Wrightstown in the 1910s, questioned Mrs. LeRoy and came to the conclusion that the boy was not Buddy. He thought that perhaps the group was on its way to see the circus in Appleton as the event had been widely advertised throughout the region.

It was not an uncommon practice for hoboes of the day to pick up boys, who they used to beg for food and clothing for them; people were more likely to give these things to a young boy than to grown men. That Buddy Schumacher may have been serving hoboes in this way seemed plausible to many police officers.

On July 30, Oshkosh residents Mr. and Mrs. Adolph Siebold said that they saw a boy matching Buddy's description with three men on a lane leading to Plummers Point, a few miles northwest of Oshkosh. The Siebolds said they saw an old man, two younger ones and a boy about eight years old near a car parked close to a field. The license plate, covered partially by mud, seemed to be a Florida plate, they said, according to an Associated Press story.

The Siebolds said they asked the group some questions and received some curt answers before the men took the boy into the car and drove toward Oshkosh. They said the boy had on a pair of overalls, wore canvas shoes and was hatless, which seemed to match up with what Buddy was wearing when he left home. The couple reported the incident to police, but no further trace of the group was found.

There was also a report of an eight-year-old boy wandering in La Crosse who was dressed in makeshift clothing. The boy was arrested by police and told conflicting stories. "He gives the name of John Rudke and says he comes from Redmond, Minnesota," La Crosse police chief John B. Weber said of the lad. "But he is unable to describe anything about Redmond or answer any questions about it. He says he is 10 years old but looks younger. He tells us his parents died and he ran away, and he has been sleeping outdoors hereabouts for several days." Descriptions exchanged over the telephone showed that this boy was not Buddy, however.

The same day, local police received a report from motorcycle patrolman M.E. Braheim of Columbia County that a lad resembling Buddy Schumacher had been seen in Lodi. The officer notified authorities that he saw a youngster dressed in overalls and showing an unkempt appearance enter a store there and buy several ice cream cones. Braheim studied a photo of Buddy that night and decided that the two were one in the same. He made a trip to Lodi to investigate further. Nothing came of this report, though.

On August 1, a boy and two men passed through Fall River in Columbia County, where Constable W.H. Field had been on the watch for Buddy. The constable questioned the men and the boy, finding out that the boy was thirteen years old and the son of one of the men he was accompanying. Yet the rumor that Buddy might be in Fall River prompted a visit from Chief Baltes anyway.

Meanwhile, Wauwatosa police discovered a "robbers' roost" in what was described as the most impregnable portion of the yunkles of the Menomonee River known as the riverbed or the river bottom about half a mile northwest of the city. The place had been known as somewhere criminals used to hide out. This area pointed to a hasty departure by members of a gang of thieves that had been harassing the neighborhood, and Chief Baltes found a large cache of food, as well as several items that had recently been reported stolen from neighboring farmhouses.

A *Milwaukee Sentinel* report at the end of July alleged that the Schumacher family had sought out a medium in a desperate attempt to gain some knowledge into what had happened to Buddy. The medium reportedly assured the family that the boy was still alive, although he was being held captive by two men.

Chapter 9

NO SIGN OF THE BOY

By the first of August, circulars bearing Buddy Schumacher's description and picture had been sent to every major city in the United States. Meanwhile, every special and regular deputy in Milwaukee County was called on to participate in a sweeping search for the boy. Undersheriff Kroening stated that if the boy was within one hundred miles, he'd be located.

Deputies were told to consider two theories: that Buddy had been kidnapped and was still alive and that he'd been killed and was lying in the yunkles northwest of Wauwatosa. Those deputies with cars searched every section of Milwaukee and Madison and all the way north to Oshkosh. Others paid particular attention to the towns along the Milwaukee Road tracks. Another crew of deputies searched the Wauwatosa yunkles thoroughly, and yet another band of deputies searched the railroad right-of-way from Wauwatosa west all the way to Brookfield. Those searching the right-of-way also searched the woods and grain and cornfields that lay near the tracks.

To make the search even more thorough, Milwaukee Road officials ordered all section foremen between Milwaukee and Portage to investigate the right-of-way and to have all section workers comb the weeds and brush near the tracks. This was also when the reward for finding Buddy was doubled to $1,000, as Art and Florence Schumacher, as well as neighbors, had become quite dejected over the failure to find the boy.

A story in the August 2 *Milwaukee Sentinel* described the mindset of the community over the crime at that time: "These neighbors of the Schumachers, fathers and mothers of children of Buddy's age, are not only ready to pay for a solution of the apparent crime, but they are preparing to demand some drastic and thorough action on the part of officials to locate the persons responsible for Buddy's disappearance and to insure safety for their own children."

Assuming that Frank Blue's story might be true, Kroening decided that the boy must have dropped out of sight off the train somewhere between about half a mile west of the swimming hole and Brookfield. It was quite possible that he'd been thrown from the train and crawled off into a nearby field, where he had not yet been located.

An eerie, heartbreaking photo was published in the *Sentinel* that day as the Schumacher family was photographed at its dinner table, with four places set. One of the places sat before an empty chair, one that had been Buddy's just over a week before. Art and Florence Schumacher sat across from each other staring at the table forlornly. Jeanette sat between them looking straight at the camera with a look that makes one wonder if she's thinking why these people have come into their home to disturb them at a time such as this.

The caption above the photo had the headline "THE VACANT CHAIR," and the caption read: "The deserted place at the table is where Arthur (Buddy) Schumacher would be if he were at home. The photograph was taken last night in the Schumacher cottage at 191 Alice Street, Wauwatosa. Mr. and Mrs. Arthur Schumacher are shown with Jeanette, aged 11, their only other child, as they gathered for the evening meal."

A later edition of the *Sentinel* on August 2 noted that a report of "confidential information" was being sent to the Wauwatosa police that would open up a new line of investigation. This information wasn't disclosed due to its nature but came about due to the reward for finding Buddy being increased. Should the information prove reliable, police said, it "might lead to sensational developments within twenty-four hours."

That information could have been the first tangible piece of potential physical evidence that came to light on August 3 when some bloody boys' clothing was found on the north side of Milwaukee. Newspaper reports differed on exactly how the evidence came to light. A United Press account reported that Patrolman Herbert Schollman found some bloodied and torn boys' knickerbockers-type trousers in a corner of a north-side Milwaukee hall. Another newspaper article, this one in the *Sentinel*, noted that the clothing was "a suit of bloodstained boys underwear" found "secreted in a hole near their home" at Holton and Locust Streets, or Locust and Bremen, just west of the Milwaukee River.

The United Press report went on to say that Schollman immediately notified headquarters, sending police, sheriff's deputies and volunteer

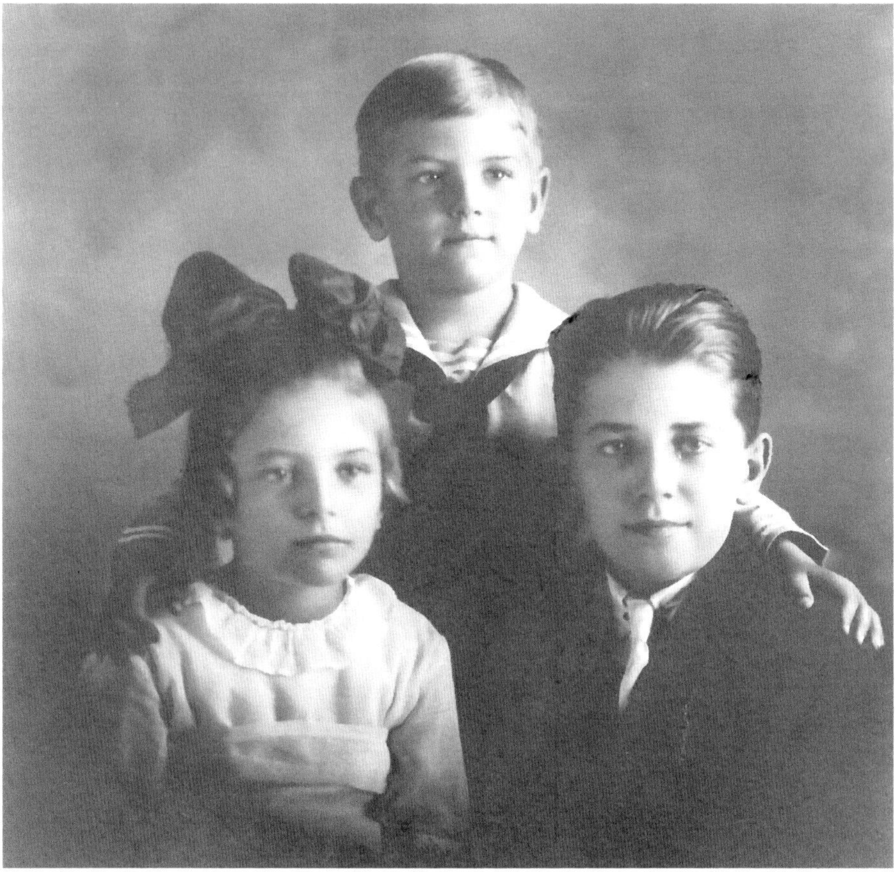

Buddy Schumacher (back) with his sister, Jeanette, and cousin, Robert Schumacher.

searchers out into the area. The *Sentinel* story noted that the clothing was determined to be Buddy Schumacher's size by Detective Kraemer, who took the clothing to the Schumacher home for possible identification. Upon seeing the clothing, however, Art Schumacher said it did not belong to his son, who was wearing no underclothing when he had left the house.

A *Milwaukee Sentinel* story of August 4 said that police put no stock in the finding of the soiled clothing. The story reported that police did not take the clothing in to the station and that it was never associated with the Schumacher case. The place where they were found was a spot used by boys to dress for swimming in the river and may have simply been discarded.

About this time, reports came in of unfamiliar boys being noticed in two locations in Wisconsin. One, in Fond du Lac, turned out to be a boy from a new family in town; the other, in Madison, turned out to belong to a family stopping at a tourist camp.

Just a day or two after sending out circulars, Police Chief Baltes announced that he would send out a second round of bulletins, this time including a more detailed description of Buddy, as well as offering the $1,000 reward. The circular was to be distributed in the states surrounding Wisconsin—Minnesota, Iowa, Illinois, Indiana and Michigan.

As theory after theory and lead after lead failed to produce Buddy, the theories and actions began to take on somewhat crazy and desperate overtones. Detective Arthur Burns, another of the officers who had been investigating the case, declared on August 3 his latest theory as to what had happened to Buddy. According to a United Press story, Burns theorized that after Buddy climbed aboard the freight train, he pulled open the ice chest hatch of a refrigerator car and jumped or fell into the car. Once within the narrow chamber, Burns said, it would have been nearly impossible for Buddy to escape. Police immediately instituted a check of all cars in the train that had passed through Wauwatosa on the day the lad vanished. Once again, this proved fruitless.

Meanwhile, Baltes decided that two draggings of the Menomonee River were not enough and ordered a third, this one farther west, upstream, in what the United Press story termed "a final effort to find the boy." Nothing was found.

A tip from tourists sent investigators to Lake Beulah, about twenty-five miles southwest of Wauwatosa, on August 4. The screams of a boy had been reported coming from a cottage there by tourists passing by on old Wisconsin State Trunk Highway 61, which appears to be the route covered now by Interstate 43. It's not clear from the *Milwaukee Sentinel* story of the next day if the report concerned the town of Lake Beulah or the lake itself, which is a few miles west of the town. Deputy John Mahoney and Detective Kraemer searched scores of cottages along the highway and talked to residents in the area. They could find no trace of the screaming boy nor anyone who had seen a strange boy in the neighborhood.

Meanwhile, a canvas shoe similar to the kind Buddy wore was found along the riverbank in Wauwatosa. The shoe was taken to Art and Florence, who declared that it did not belong to their son.

The next day, Buddy's relatives, believing that the Menomonee River may yet be the key to the mystery, started a movement to have the water blasted. According to a *Sentinel* story in the August 6 paper, they thought that the boy may have been held on the river bottom by a snag or that a false bottom or hole may have taken the body out of reach of draggers. The plan was to have an experienced dynamiter explode several charges in parts of the river deep enough to conceal a body. At the time, there were three deep holes within half a mile of the place where Buddy dropped from sight.

It was said that the river sometimes did not give up its dead, according to an August 6 story in the *Milwaukee Sentinel*. Wauwatosa police pointed to the drowning "some years ago" of Lawrence Brennan, son of attorney Martin Brennan, at about the same spot that Buddy was thought to have disappeared. The younger Brennan's body was never recovered.

That day, two more reports of boys in strange situations reached detectives. Two women and a boy asked assistance of a farmer on the Kilbourn Road and were subsequently questioned. But the women—Mrs. Mathilda Brechtold and Mrs. Rose Milford of Milwaukee—said they'd been "ejected" from the automobile of a friend who was taking them for a ride. The boy was Mrs. Brechtold's son, Gustave, age eight. Another report of a strange boy on the south side of Milwaukee was investigated, but to no avail.

Two days later, the quarry east of Hawley Road and south of State Street was dynamited after a painter reported to Undersheriff Kroening the night before that on the day the Schumacher boy disappeared he'd seen a boy about Buddy's age, size and description playing about the "treacherous" quarry. The water in the quarry was said to reach a depth of thirty feet in some places, and it was believed that the low temperature of the water would prevent the boy's body from rising.

The same *Milwaukee Sentinel* story said that a night watchman named Matt Kraemer at a Fond du Lac drugstore told police that he saw a boy matching Buddy's description in the back seat of a car that was heading north. The vehicle, with Illinois plates, also held "three ill-kept men of foreign appearance." Once again, nothing came of this report.

At the end of the search's second week, Chicago police and authorities in all the towns between Chicago and Milwaukee were advised to be on the lookout for a touring car in which Buddy was thought to be riding. Louis Glowecki of Cudahy, a southern suburb of Milwaukee, was waiting for a streetcar near Pulaski Avenue when he said that he'd seen what he believed to be a man dressed in women's clothes with the boy. Glowecki said that the boy looked out of a stalled car at him and called to him, "Won't you please help me." As Glowecki started toward the car, the automobile started and roared off, he said.

"The man—or maybe it was a woman, but it looked like a man—said something to him and drove off in the machine, headed south," Glowecki was quoted as saying in a *Sentinel* story. He said that the car had an Illinois license plate and that the boy, about Buddy's age, was dressed in khaki overalls. Once again, nothing came of it.

Chapter 10

THE HUNT GRINDS TO A HALT

The stress of not knowing what had happened to her son, and battling the fears that he might be dead, took a great toll on Florence Schumacher. After being overcome with grief and exhaustion after just a few sleepless days and nights of searching for Buddy, Florence spent virtually the next two weeks in her home, attended to by her older sister, Gertrude Brown.

Florence's desperation was detailed in a story in the August 7 *Sentinel*, headlined, "HER'S THE HORROR OF NOT KNOWING; SHE CAN ONLY WAIT AND PRAY." A second headline read, "SOME GRIEVE IN THE KNOWLEDGE OF THEIR LOVED ONES' DEATHS; MRS. SCHUMACHER IS DENIED EVEN THAT SOLACE."

The story was accompanied by a photo of Florence sitting at home, holding Buddy's baby shoe in one hand while her head rested in the other hand. Under the photo ran the caption: "It is just a baby shoe, dilapidated and almost worn through. But it has become Mrs. Florence Schumacher's most treasured possession. The shoe belonged to her son, Arthur, now 8 years old, who vanished mysteriously two weeks ago today. Fondling the things he wore and looking at his toys strengthens her in the intuitive confidence that the boy is still alive and that some time he will again be a member of the family group, Mrs. Schumacher said."

Here is the story in its entirety:

THE MOTHER OF SORROW!

You may fittingly call Mrs. A.M. Schumacher that, for few mothers—even those who have watched the angel of death summon a child, have trod the

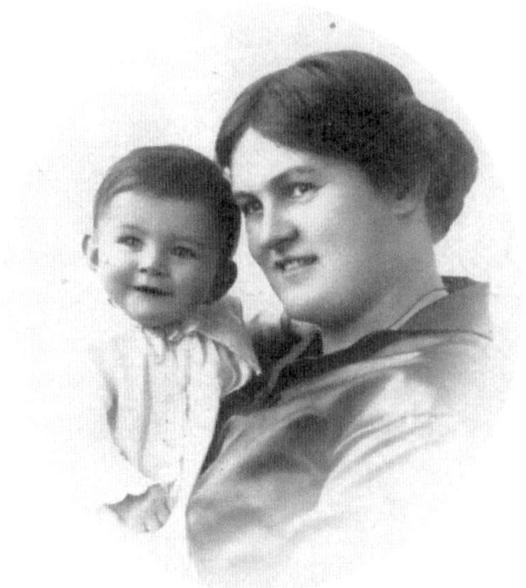

Florence Schumacher with her daughter, Jeanette.

Golgotha (also known as Calvary, site of the crucifixion of Jesus Christ) that she is traveling.

In a modest, but immaculate home at 191 Alice street, in Wauwatosa, she is sitting and waiting. Always waiting! Praying! Hoping! Waiting for some news, any news of her boy, Arthur. Praying that no harm has befallen him. Hoping, always hoping, that the next minute will bring him tripping up the stairs.

It is just two weeks today since she kissed him and saw him run to his play.

In these two weeks she has lived and experienced an anguish that seems to have been of a century's duration. She is torn by an interminable suspense, her mind reaching out vainly for answers to torturing questions.

Is He Dead?

"Is he dead?"

"If he is alive, is he being treated well?"

"What adventure has taken him from his mother and home?"

"Is he trying to get back, encountering strange and unthinkable hardships?"

"Has he succumbed to injuries, suffering in some forsaken spot without attendance and the touch of a comforting hand?"

Suffering has left its mark in her face. Yet she is a brave woman. Even her sister, Mrs. Brown, who has come to be with her in her hour of trial, and who never leaves her side, marvels at the fortitude that keeps her on her feet, caring for her shattered family.

She has cried. Oh, yes. Her eyes allow that, in fact the tears have practically harrowed grooves in her face. Even now, after two weeks of weeping, the tears well up unexpectedly. But Mrs. Schumacher controls them. Here is that silent, wracking grief that is harder to watch than the hysterical kind. It has no outlet so it must carry its sharp pain still more deeply inward.

Anything to Find Boy

Always a quiet woman who has never sought the limelight, who has looked with true American repugnance upon notoriety, she is willing to do anything that may lead to the most trifling clew. If interest, lagging in a public that forgets all too soon, must be re-awakened, she is willing to sacrifice her feelings. She will talk, even though every word is a new stab in her heart, if talking will lead to some new discovery of Arthur's whereabouts.

She will bring out the baby shoe, sacred to a mother, and let others see her fondle it, if that picture will awaken a response some place that will lead to the discovery of Arthur's whereabouts.

Amid it all she bears up wonderfully. The two weeks of strain might have broken another woman. Not Mrs. Schumacher. There is not even a single nervous action nor one protest against an unkind fate to betray the suffering those fourteen days have extracted.

True, she has one source of comfort, an unfailing source.

"I don't know what I would do," she said quietly but firmly, "if I were an unbeliever and had no God to turn to. In prayer I have found the faith to believe and the courage to keep on. I am a member of the Mount Olive Lutheran church and the members have been so kind about joining in general prayers for Arthur's recovery.

"I believe other churches have also prayed. I hope that every one who is at all religious will overlook the differences in one faith and another and add their prayers to those said."

Mrs. Schumacher does not dwell on the various angles that have entered the case since the disappearance of 8 year old Arthur has been reported. She just wants him. The pretty little home that is the reward of years of thrift she would gladly exchange for her boy—her baby.

"The house, anything we have, we would be only too glad to hand it over if it meant his safe return," is the way she puts it.

Just how a new font of hope has been awakened by the fact that a traveling man believes he saw Arthur on a freight car grinning sheepishly at the admonishing finger the traveling man held up, as much as to say that, he did not relish being there but was too afraid to jump off. In the way she tells it you gather a good picture of the kind and sane upbringing that Arthur has had.

Today, as she has for the last thirteen days, Mrs. Schumacher will stay at home, waiting for news. The person who furnished the clue that may lead to Arthur will never be forgotten by her. And even the people who think of her plight and whisper a prayer for heaven to conduct the little boy safely to her, will win her gratitude.

After two weeks of searching, one school of thought said that Buddy may have passed beyond the Wisconsin border and into Minnesota, the Dakotas, Montana, Idaho or Washington. The Salvation Army, which operated a bureau for missing persons, forwarded Buddy's description to all of its posts in the United States.

By the middle of August, the nationwide appeal that had included 2,500 descriptive circulars had brought many reports of boys thought to be Buddy. One such lead came from a Fort Wayne, Indiana woman on August 15. She said she had seen a boy riding through town on a tourist's truck with an Illinois license plate that might be the lad. But this lead, and all others, never produced the boy. Hope for finding the boy alive was almost nil, and hope for finding him at all was fading fast.

Some thought that there might be a break in the case in late August with what appeared to be a confession. A note supposedly describing Buddy's death was found written in pencil on a piece of oak driftwood smoothed with a penknife in a pool of water in a vacant lot near what is now Florida and south First Streets just south of downtown Milwaukee. Five boys at play, just after noon on August 27, found the note in an area that was described in a *Sentinel* article as "a district that is frequented by the dregs of humanity."

The note said: "I killed the Schumacher kid for revenge. I tied a stone around his neck and threw him off the government pier near the quarry out there. You'll never find me, but you can take him if you drag the lake on the north side of the pier." The *Sentinel* story reported that the note was signed with the name "Tommy Sutton," although the *Journal* noted that the signature was illegible, and it was not known if it was initials or a full name.

Police came to the conclusion that the note was a hoax for a few reasons. First of all, they figured that the wood had been placed in the water just a short time before. Also, the government pier was in Lake Michigan and nowhere near a quarry. However, the pier referred to in the note, Detective Bruno Zellmer thought, might be the pier in the Menomonee River near Blackridge. Authorities figured that the message was written by a boy or fisherman "with a distorted sense of humor," according to the *Wauwatosa News*.

However, almost as soon as this clue was dismissed, authorities did a 180-degree turn and saw it as genuine. Hope of finding the body was announced with a large headline across the top of the front page of the August 30 *Milwaukee Sentinel and Milwaukee Telegram* that blared "LAKE CLEW REVIVES BOY HUNT." After reading what the note had said in the newspaper, quarry man William Manegold recalled that there was a pier at the old stone quarry at Belgium, Wisconsin, where he used to be employed. He went to the Milwaukee County sheriff's office on August 29 and described the scene at Belgium, about forty miles north of Milwaukee not far from Lake Michigan.

Manegold then took Sheriff Reichenbach and Undersheriff Kroening to the pier. The *Journal* pinpointed the location of this quarry a little more definitely, putting it at a lake at Sucker Brook, about two miles north of Port Washington and five miles south of Belgium. Sucker Brook drains into Lake Michigan, and there is a small lake not far from the shore.

The oak that the note was scrawled on looked like it very well could have come from the pier at Belgium, it was reported. Meanwhile, a farming couple that lived near the pier, Mr. and Mrs. Enazio Zitella, said that they had seen a man hanging about the pier for many hours one afternoon and evening about four or five weeks previous, which would have been around the time of the Schumacher disappearance. The Zitellas' daughter, Ida, also said that she saw the man and told the sheriff that he was there until a late hour that night, sitting alongside a fire that he had built.

Another local man corroborated the Zitellas' story. Retired farmer J.B. Krier, who spent many of his hours fishing at the lake, reported that he'd seen a man with a small boy on the pier about four or five weeks before this. He couldn't furnish any descriptions because he said that he was a good two blocks away from the pier at the time.

The quarry had been abandoned for five or six years, and the pier was in a desolate spot, where a person would not have been seen except by perhaps a few of the farmers who lived nearby. That was enough evidence for the Belgium quarry lake to be dragged for many hours, and the search continued on into the dark. The plan was to hire a diver if the dragging did

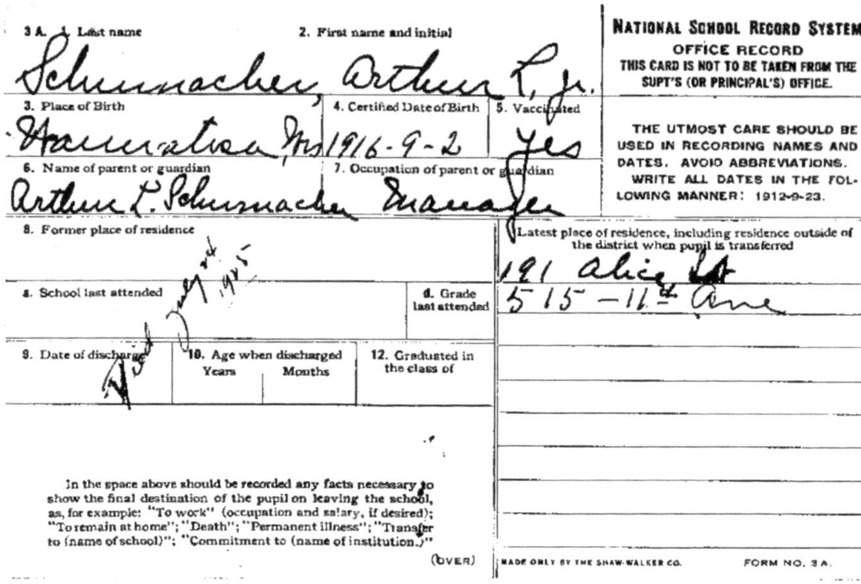

3 A. 1. Last name: Schumacher | 2. First name and initial: Arthur L., Jr.

3. Place of Birth: Wauwatosa, Wis. | 4. Certified Date of Birth: 1916-9-2 | 5. Vaccinated: Yes

6. Name of parent or guardian: Arthur L. Schumacher | 7. Occupation of parent or guardian: Manager

8. Former place of residence

a. School last attended | d. Grade last attended

9. Date of discharge: 24th July 1925 | 10. Age when discharged: Years, Months | 12. Graduated in the class of

In the space above should be recorded any facts necessary to show the final destination of the pupil on leaving the school, as, for example: "To work" (occupation and salary, if desired); "To remain at home"; "Death"; "Permanent illness"; "Transfer to (name of school)"; "Commitment to (name of institution.)"

(OVER)

NATIONAL SCHOOL RECORD SYSTEM
OFFICE RECORD
THIS CARD IS NOT TO BE TAKEN FROM THE SUPT'S (OR PRINCIPAL'S) OFFICE.

THE UTMOST CARE SHOULD BE USED IN RECORDING NAMES AND DATES. AVOID ABBREVIATIONS. WRITE ALL DATES IN THE FOLLOWING MANNER: 1912-9-23.

Latest place of residence, including residence outside of the district when pupil is transferred

191 Alice St.
515 – 11th Ave.

MADE ONLY BY THE SHAW-WALKER CO. FORM NO. 3 A.

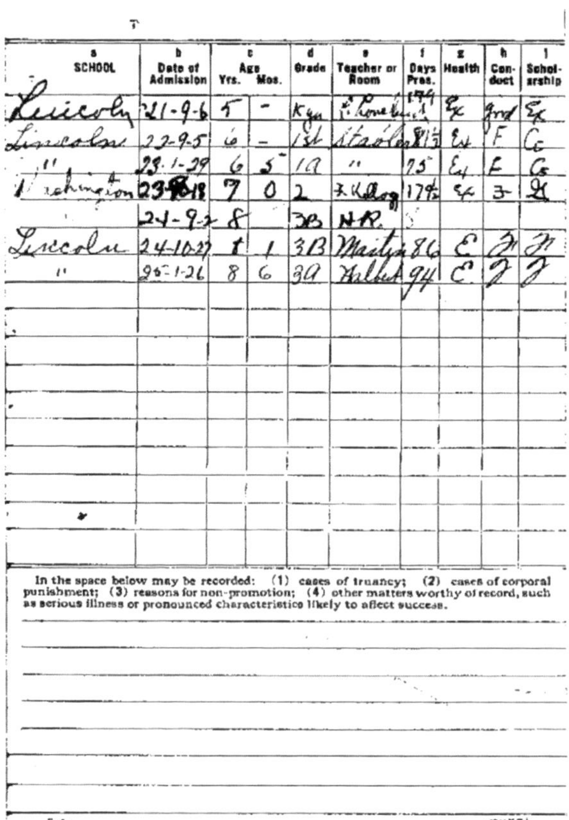

a SCHOOL	b Date of Admission	c Age Yrs.	Mos.	d Grade	e Teacher or Room	f Days Pres.	g Health	h Conduct	i Scholarship
Lincoln	21-9-6	5	–	Kg	[illegible]	179	Ex	Good	Ex
Lincoln	22-9-5	6	–	1st	[illegible]	81½	Ex	F	G
"	23-1-29	6	5	1A	"	75	Ex	F	G
Washington	23-9-18	7	0	2	[illegible]	179½	Ex	3	G
	24-9-2	8		3B	N.R.				
Lincoln	24-10-27	8	1	3B	Martin	86	E	F	F
"	25-1-26	8	6	3A	[illegible]	94	E	F	F

In the space below may be recorded: (1) cases of truancy; (2) cases of corporal punishment; (3) reasons for non-promotion; (4) other matters worthy of record, such as serious illness or pronounced characteristics likely to affect success.

3 A. (OVER)

Above: Buddy Schumacher's permanent school records shows the addresses where he lived and notes his official date of death, July 24, 1925.

Left: The back of Buddy Schumacher's school record notes that he attended Lincoln School for kindergarten, first and third grade, but attended Washington School during second grade.

not produce a body. The pier was dilapidated, and stones were falling out from the pilings, making the task of dragging the lake very difficult.

Even though police thought that the note on the old piece of oak might have some truth to it, they doubted that the killing was done for revenge, if in fact the boy was really thrown from the pier. Authorities were still of the opinion that Buddy had been lured away by a degenerate. Because the driftwood was found in a ramshackle area of Milwaukee, authorities were strengthened in their belief that the message was not a hoax. The dragging of the Sucker Brook lake did not produce a body, however.

The Wauwatosa Quarry was dynamited for a second time on September 5. The quarry of the Manegold Stone Company at Hawley Road was blasted again and flooded in an attempt to find the boy on Labor Day, September 7. The quarry was also dragged for several hours after one hundred pounds of dynamite was set off in seventy-foot depths. But once again these attempts failed to produce a body, like all the other attempts before them. With no other clues, the hunt for Buddy grounded virtually to a halt.

What would have been Buddy's ninth birthday passed by on September 2 without any news of his whereabouts, and as the weather started to cool a bit, most Wauwatosans were getting back to their normal lives. Children went back to school for another year on September 8, the day after Labor Day. Buddy's sister, Jeanette, entered Lincoln School for sixth grade. But this fall, her little brother did not join her.

Less than one week later, however, the town of Wauwatosa would once again be turned upside down, this time as everyone's worst fears were finally realized.

Chapter 11

THE BODY IS FINALLY FOUND

While attending church services in Milwaukee the morning of Sunday, September 13, Milwaukee resident Joseph V. Vozar made the decision to drive to Wauwatosa to hunt mushrooms after the service. Vozar started searching for mushrooms in some woods near both Underwood Creek and the railroad tracks just a little northwest of the spot where Buddy had last been seen. The property was at the south end of C.A. Koepfler's farm, the entrance of which was probably located between 102nd and 104th Streets on North Avenue today. The woods, said to be about a quarter mile south of the farmhouse, were reported to have a heavy growth of weeds and brush and is now most likely just a little southwest of the Hansen Park Golf Course.

Despite this being a traditionally good time of year for mushroom hunting in the area, Vozar was having no luck. He was about to leave at eleven o'clock when he decided to give it one more shot, pushing his way through a closely grown thicket beneath an arch formed by two oak trees leaning together not far from a cow path that led to the Koepfler farmhouse. There, he stumbled over a small body, lying facedown with arms outstretched. Vozar saw that the clothing on the body had been torn, and that the body had badly decomposed.

Figuring that he'd probably stumbled on the Schumacher boy but not knowing for certain, Vozar seriously considered not telling anyone what he'd found, as he didn't want to be drawn into the case, according to a story in the following day's *Milwaukee Sentinel*. In fact, he drove all the way home without telling anyone and ate his dinner before changing his mind and telling his son, Emil. "The first thing I saw was the blue overalls and then the white canvas shoes," Vozar later said. "That was enough for me, and I hurried from the place as fast as I could."

Vozar then called his neighbor, Dennis Uradnicek. Along with his son and his neighbor, Vozar returned to the place where he'd seen the body. They took along with them a copy of Buddy's photo that had been widely published in newspapers and circulars for close to two months. It wasn't easy to find the spot again; Vozar said that it took twenty minutes to locate the body this time.

The three compared Buddy's photo and description with the body and were sure that they'd found him. After viewing the body again, Vozar reported what his party had discovered to Sergeant Adolph Hedhke at the Wauwatosa Police Department. Hedhke took some patrolmen out to the scene and determined the body to be the boy whom the entire city, as well as many in outlaying areas, had searched for so intently for the past seven weeks. They said that the clothing was most likely torn in a struggle but that the condition of the body made it impossible to determine the cause of death at that time. Shortly after Deputy Coroner Walter Krueger arrived on the scene, the body was taken to the police department and later to the county morgue. Four sheriff's deputies were immediately dispatched to the area to search for clues. But their efforts yielded nothing.

Police tried to contact Art and Florence to deliver the news that their son's body had finally been found. But Florence's brothers, Fred and Edwin Armstrong, who were living with the Schumachers at the time, told authorities that Buddy's parents had gone to visit relatives for the day in North Prairie. In the meantime, Fred and Edwin officially identified their nephew's body.

The area where the body was found was one that had been searched at least a dozen times. And since the clump of bushes was in plain sight, and the body could be seen from a few yards away, many could not believe that the body hadn't been found earlier. The owner of the property where the boy was found was astounded to hear the news.

"They found him in those woods?" questioned Koepfler, who was not home when the body was found but arrived the following day. "Why, the sheriff's men and the Boy Scouts were over my property several times. The place must have been searched a dozen times."

The man who managed Koepfler's farm was shocked, too. Otto Reinholz, his wife and some friends had hiked through those same woods a few weeks previous. "We were within twenty feet of the boy," Reinholz said. "We sat on the grass talking so close to the spot that I could have tossed a twig into those bushes. I remember that one of the men in the party walked through those very bushes."

When Art and Florence finally got word that their son's body had been found, they were obviously distraught, but at least the uncertainty was gone. "Oh, I'm glad it's over," Florence was quoted as saying in the *Wauwatosa News*. "The waiting and thinking with nothing we could do. It's good to know what became of Arthur, even if it is terrible…I did hope—I had half an idea that he might be living. I wonder if he could have been lying there while all those people searched right in those woods. I wonder if he could not have been left there later than that, after the searching was over."

The boy's father expressed similar sentiments and thanked those who had helped with the search. "It is a blow to know that he is dead, but it is better than to go on fearing and worrying and never knowing what became of him," Art said. "Now, we can bury him and we will know where he is. I wonder if anyone knows how much that means to us."

Police left little doubt that Buddy had been mistreated and murdered. They pointed out that had he been injured after falling from a train, it would be almost impossible to imagine the boy crawling a quarter mile from the tracks. And the body was described as mutilated in addition to being decomposed.

As one might imagine, Monday's daily newspapers in Milwaukee splashed the news of the boy's discovery all over their front pages, and the *Sentinel* did it up to the hilt. The morning paper's two-deck headline, with bold capital letters more than an inch tall, screamed, "Schumacher Boy Murdered; Mutilated Body Is Found" in its Latest Edition. At the very top of the page was a box stretching across the top of the entire page, with "$1000" printed in even larger type, denoting the offer of that amount as a reward. Inside the box was the following: "The *Sentinel* offers a reward of $1000 for the apprehension of the slayer of little Arthur Schumacher. Every possible effort must be made to discover and bring to justice the perpetrator of this atrocious crime."

Besides a story on the discovery of the body, the *Sentinel*'s coverage also included a large photo of Buddy, the same that had been published shortly after the boy disappeared. There was also a timeline of the investigation, featuring key dates from the time when the boy disappeared until the body was found. There was also a photo of four deputies—Walter McCaigue, Alex Fitzgerald, Art Wilcox and Jack Kenehan—at the site where the body was found. McCaigue is photographed pointing to a spot in the brush. A dashed white line leads from the McCaigue's finger to a large white X on

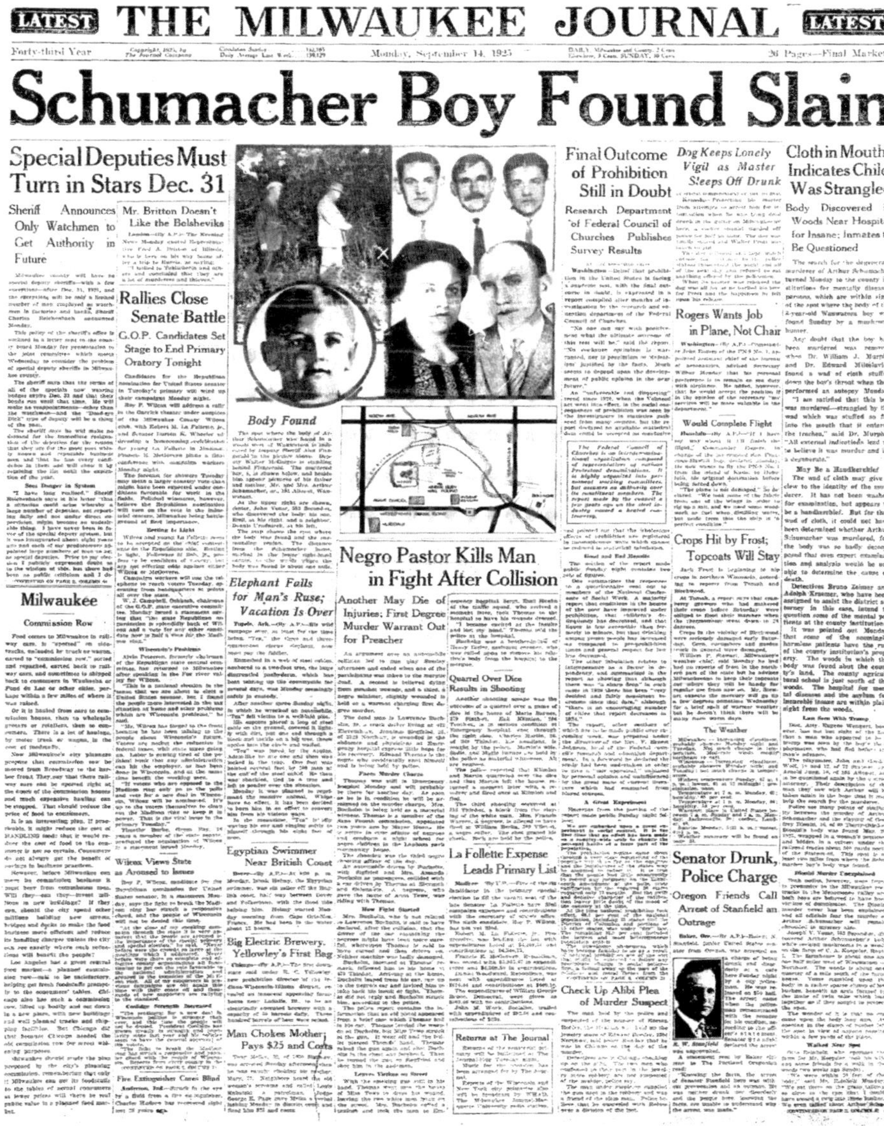

LATEST THE MILWAUKEE JOURNAL LATEST

Forty-third Year — Monday, September 14, 1925 — 26 Pages—Final Markets

Schumacher Boy Found Slain

Special Deputies Must Turn in Stars Dec. 31

Sheriff Announces Only Watchmen to Get Authority in Future

Mr. Britton Doesn't Like the Bolsheviks

Rallies Close Senate Battle

G.O.P. Candidates Set Stage to End Primary Oratory Tonight

Milwaukee

Commission Row

Body Found

Final Outcome of Prohibition Still in Doubt

Research Department of Federal Council of Churches Publishes Survey Results

Dog Keeps Lonely Vigil as Master Sleeps Off Drunk

Rogers Wants Job in Plane, Not Chair

Would Complete Flight

Cloth in Mouth Indicates Child Was Strangled

Body Discovered in Woods Near Hospital for Insane; Inmates to Be Questioned

May Be a Handkerchief

Negro Pastor Kills Man in Fight After Collision

Another May Die of Injuries; First Degree Murder Warrant Out for Preacher

Elephant Fails for Man's Ruse; Vacation Is Over

Quarrel Over Dice Results in Shooting

Crops Hit by Frost; Topcoats Will Stay

The Weather

Egyptian Swimmer Near British Coast

Big Electric Brewery, Yellowley's First Bag

Man Chokes Mother; Pays $25 and Costs

La Follette Expense Leads Primary List

Senator Drunk, Police Charge

Oregon Friends Call Arrest of Stanfield an Outrage

Check Up Alibi Plea of Murder Suspect

Returns at The Journal

Wilcox Views State as Aroused to Issues

Fire Extinguisher Cures Blind

"Schumacher Boy Found Slain," *Milwaukee Journal*, September 14, 1925.

the ground, both having been drawn in by someone on the newspaper staff. Photos of Joseph Vozar, his son and Dennis Uradnicek were also printed. Finally, a crude, far-from-scale map tried to indicate the location of where the body was found and relate it to the location of the Schumacher home, the county institutions and other nearby landmarks.

The *Milwaukee Sentinel* also devoted plenty of space to the news that the boy's body had finally been located, including four photos and a map on the front page, along with the large headline, "SCHUMACHER BOY FOUND SLAIN."

The *Journal*'s photos included one of Deputy Alex Fitzgerald pointing to the spot in the woods where the body was found, with a white X marking the spot. Photos of Buddy, as well as his mother and father, were also published, as was a picture of Vozar with his son and neighbor flanking him, with all three in white shirts and ties.

Although not perfect, the *Journal*'s map depicting the spot where the body was found was much neater and probably more accurate than the *Sentinel*'s. It showed the Koepfler farmhouse on North Avenue, with a path leading southeast from the house, across a small bridge that spanned the river and south past a cornfield. Once past the cornfield, the path turned directly west into the wooded area. The Milwaukee Road tracks ran through what was Koepfler's property. Underwood Creek, a tributary of the Menomonee River, follows the tracks through this area quite closely, and the body was apparently found in an area fairly close to Wisconsin Lutheran College's new football stadium, near where U.S. Highway 45 crosses over Underwood Parkway, a road that was not there in those days. From the spot the body was found, one could easily see the Milwaukee Aggie School to south by southeast and the county insane asylum to the southeast.

The autopsy was performed at 9:00 a.m. the day after the body was found by Coroner Henry Grudemann and Doctors Edward Miloslavich and William J. Murphy. Due to the condition of the body, it was determined that Buddy had died shortly after he had disappeared. The procedure also found the likely cause of death: a wadded-up cotton cloth, perhaps a handkerchief, had been shoved so far down Buddy's throat that it had entered his trachea.

"GAG MAY MARK BOY'S SLAYER" read the headline across the top of the front page of the *Sentinel* on September 15. What turned out to indeed be a handkerchief was thought to provide the clues that might finally lead to Buddy's assailant. The story started with the usual dramatic writing that the *Sentinel* had employed throughout the case:

> *A stained linen handkerchief which choked the life from Arthur (Buddie) Schumacher, may lead to the capture of the atrocious murderer.*
>
> *Found wedged tightly into the Wauwatosa boy's mouth, it told the story of his death; taken from the place of its deadly mission, it may point an accusing finger at its owner.*

> *In any event, it stood out last night as the sole tangible clew in the tragic death of the 8-year-old school boy who ran whistling from his yard into the clutches of a lurking degenerate.*

Dr. Murphy agreed with the basics of that assessment. "All external indications lead us to believe it was a murder and by a degenerate," he stated to both Milwaukee papers.

The writer of this story—bylines on news stories in this time period were rare, so nobody knows who wrote most of them—got a little carried away with the amount of knowledge that could be gleaned from the evidence. The story went on to suggest that it was apparent that Buddy had been lured into the brush by false pretense before being struck down by his captor:

> *The large handkerchief was then jammed into his mouth to silence his outcrys and while his life was ebbing, he was outraged. Certain it is that the little school boy never had a chance for his life.*
>
> *His assailant, in the excitement of his lust, crowded the cruel gag so far back into the boy's mouth that both throat and nasal passages were stopped up. It is declared likely that unconsciousness and then death followed quickly.*

Meanwhile, the coroner suggested that Vozar be given a reward of $1,000 for finding the body since the promise of such a reward had never been publicly withdrawn. However, Art Schumacher said that the $1,000 originally offered for Buddy's return "dead or alive" had later been changed to the "safe return" of Buddy. Later, the Wauwatosa Commercial Association voted that Vozar be given $250, even though Vozar requested nothing.

It was said that the case reminded police of the slaying of Godfrey Dionizi, a fourteen-year-old Milwaukee boy whose body was found in March 1923 wrapped in a woman's petticoat and hidden in a culvert under the railroad tracks about three hundred yards north of State Street. That spot was about two miles from where Buddy's body was found. Police noted that both bodies had been located near the Milwaukee Road tracks and the Menomonee River and that both boys were believed to have been the victims of degenerates. The Dionizi murder was never explained; officials hoped that they would not come to the same conclusion in the Schumacher case.

With Buddy's body having been found, the investigation now switched gears. No longer were authorities trying to find a missing boy; they were now charged with finding a discovered boy's killer. Police immediately suspected that a degenerate or inmate of the nearby hospital for the insane committed the act. Chief Baltes said that all suspects who had previously been questioned in the case would be brought into the Wauwatosa Police Department for more questioning.

Three homeless men who had been questioned shortly after Buddy disappeared but released due to lack of evidence were brought back in for examination. One, whose sanity had been said to be in question, was found camping in "crude fashion" near the place where the body was found. Another, found on the railroad tracks near where Buddy was last seen, was unable to give an account of himself. He had borrowed a razor at the county institutions and had shaved off what was believed to be a mustache in the woods. A third suspect was said to be a religious fanatic, wandering about the countryside, selling religious booklets and begging.

The district attorney centered his investigation almost immediately on a hobo called "The Dane," a man who had been described by another hobo as "a degenerate fully capable of so foul a crime as the murder of Arthur Schumacher," according to the September 15 *Milwaukee Sentinel.* This other hobo, who had served time in several prisons, went to Wengert with the idea to seek The Dane, who was said to have been living in the railroad yunkles outside Wauwatosa about the time Buddy went missing. The informant said that The Dane was now in Portage and was on his way to Duluth, Minnesota.

Meanwhile, Detectives Zellmer and Kramer were dispatched to the county institutions for the mentally diseased, a short distance southeast of where the body was found, to talk to the "prisoners" who had records of "perverse behavior" and also those who had been allowed to freely roam the grounds. Many of the prisoners, they found out, were known as "trusties" and were permitted outside the grounds. Detectives also interviewed a score of neighbors, trying to determine if anyone had a suspicion in the case, to no avail. In the short time police spent rounding up these persons of interest, at least four more cases of children being molested or attacked in Wauwatosa or the vicinity were reported.

Decomposition of Buddy's body was so great that had there been more evidence of foul play at one time, it had been erased by this time. And with the forensic limitations of the day (fingerprinting was still pretty much in its infancy, and DNA testing was generations off), the evidence consisted mainly of what Buddy's pals saw and the handkerchief.

It wasn't long before all the evidence pointed to one man.

Chapter 12

AN ARREST IS MADE

Buddy Schumacher's funeral was conducted at his home on Alice Street at 2:00 p.m. two days after his body was found. Reverend William Dallman, pastor at Mount Olive Lutheran Church, officiated. Four of Buddy's friends, reported to be his closest friends, were named honorary pallbearers: Robert Behnke, William Krueger, Austin Sprague and Carl Diekarske. Mrs. Moore, a member of the Mount Olive quartette singing group, sang two songs during the service and another at the cemetery.

A total of fifty relatives and friends crowded into the house on what the *Milwaukee Sentinel* described as a day "beneath dark, hovering clouds and with the chill of fall in the air." When the services ended, Dallman led the flower-decked coffin out the front door and down the stairs to the street, where the procession formed to head up the hill toward the Wauwatosa Cemetery, where Buddy was lowered to his final resting place on a knoll surrounded by pine trees.

The *Milwaukee Sentinel*'s coverage of the funeral noted, "High on the cemetery noll, overlooking the scene of his childhood, relatives and friends gathered to bid adieu to the blue eyed, fair haired school boy who went to his death, the victim of one of Milwaukee county's most revolting crimes. Mother, father, and sister stood by, all but overcome with grief, as the white coffin, banked with flowers from friends and strangers alike, was gently lowered into the grave."

Two carloads of flowers were heaped on the grave, according to a *Milwaukee Sentinel* story, but only the white gloves worn by the honorary pallbearers and a few roses and carnations rested on the coffin.

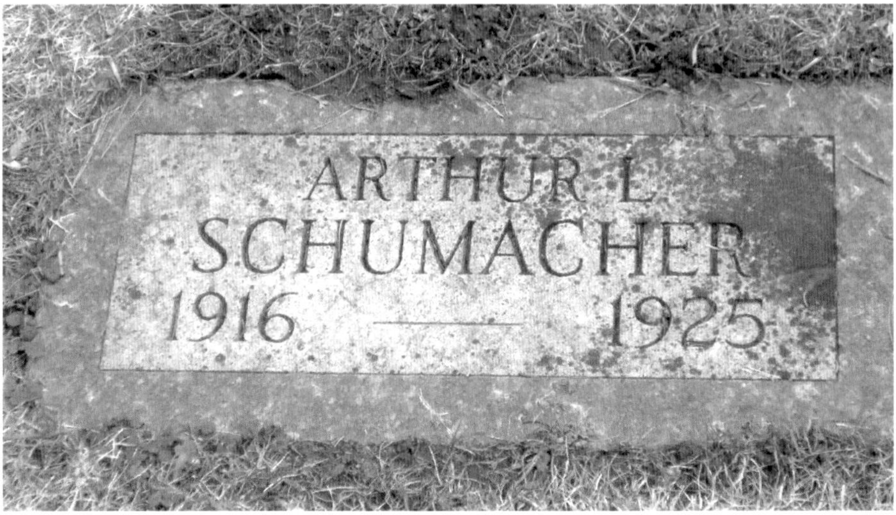

Buddy Schumacher's grave stands near the highest point in Wauwatosa Cemetery.

The *Sentinel*'s story painted Buddy's mother as someone who had been pretty much cried out by the time of the funeral. "She grieved quietly, as though a great pent-up force of emotion had been spent during the long weeks of waiting, and if not then, at the final blow which came when the body was discovered Sunday in the open grave of brush and weeds."

After returning from the cemetery, Art expressed his emotions to the paper: "If it was to be this way, it is better for his mother and us all that we could have him back now and bury him near to us."

The first order of business in finding Buddy's killer was to examine the murder weapon. The handkerchief stuffed down Buddy's throat was about four by four inches square and so stained that laundry marks or initials that may have been present on the cloth were invisible. A pathologist, Dr. William Miloslavich, put the handkerchief through a bleaching solution to whiten it and then put the handkerchief under a microscope to search for any distinguishing marks. During his examination, Miloslavich found that the letter "A" had been embroidered on it. When that initial "A" was found, authorities were inclined to believe this may have been Art Schumacher's handkerchief, but that turned out not to be the case.

Miloslavich took photographs of the handkerchief in Buddy's jaws with the prints to be used at the inquest and later at a trial, assuming that someone would be charged with the crime. He noted that there were no bone fractures and no other injury that could be determined.

"In about 7,000 cases of post mortem examination in my experience," Miloslavich was quoted as saying, "I don't believe I have ever had a more incriminating piece of evidence. The boy might have lived had the handkerchief not been crowded so far down in his mouth. It closed the trachea, causing suffocation."

The same day that Buddy was laid to rest, his companions were called into the district attorney's office to view a lineup of men arrested recently in the area. Among them was Edward Vreeland, who had been arrested as a vagrant just two days after Buddy disappeared. Vreeland had been camping out earlier in the summer near where Buddy's body was found, getting by on a diet of herbs, fruits, berries, fish and frogs. Vreeland had also been identified as someone who had given local boys trouble. In fact, he'd been tagged as a guard for a nearby hobo camp and admitted to have lived in the Koepfler woods "for some weeks."

Questioned at the time regarding Buddy's disappearance, Vreeland had professed ignorance of any connection with the case. He was arraigned in district court at the time and sentenced to sixty days in the house of correction for vagrancy. However, he didn't start that sentence for at least a week as his precarious existence in the woods was said to have left him in poor physical condition, requiring a stay in the emergency hospital before being committed to prison.

At the time he was originally picked up, Vreeland didn't give much insight into his personal life, although he did say that he was forty-five years old and that he was estranged from his wife, who was living in Chicago. Vreeland said that he had come to Milwaukee in 1918 and had lived at four different residences. Information gleaned from city directories, census reports and Ancestry.com seems to back up Vreeland's claims and gives additional background into his life.

It appears as though Edward Garret Vreeland was born on January 19, 1880, in Illinois, the youngest of five children born to Garret C. and Lydia Ann Eames Harris Vreeland. His father died when he was about ten years old, and it appears that he often went by "Eddy." He broke his right leg when he was twelve years old, according to his draft registration card that was filed in Milwaukee in 1918.

It's difficult to pinpoint where Vreeland went from the time he left his parents' home in Big Grove, Illinois, until he ended up in Milwaukee in 1918. But it looks like he was living in downtown Chicago in 1900. He married Bertha Devlin, and they had two children: Valeria, born in 1909 in St. Louis, and Victoria, born in 1911 in Chicago.

By 1918, Vreeland had left his family and moved to Milwaukee, with his first address perhaps the Hartford Hotel at the corner of Biddle (now Kilbourn) and Market Streets, in the heart of the downtown area. He was a trucking laborer working for the Chicago and North Western Railroad Company, according to his draft card.

Milwaukee city directories note that Vreeland rented rooms in cheap Milwaukee hotels or rooming houses for a few years. The 1921 directory lists him as an office manager of Grain Juice Company, most likely a former brewery that was now producing near beer and soft drinks, in downtown Milwaukee. But no job was listed for him in 1922, the last city directory in which Edward Vreeland appeared. He most likely caught on as a lodger at various houses until the spring of 1925, when he said he decided he didn't want to continue working nor pay rent. So, he took up the vagabond's lifestyle.

After Buddy's body was found, the detectives who had arrested Vreeland earlier—Deputies John Kenehan and Edward Siepman—recalled that he'd been picked up in the same general vicinity as where Buddy's body lay.

When Buddy's friends viewed the lineup of men, Arnold Yunk and John Wolf picked out Vreeland as the man who had approached them on the day Buddy was last seen, even though Yunk was the one who had said he did not recognize Vreeland the first time the man was apprehended. A United Press story noted that the boys "expressed conviction" that this was the man. The *Wauwatosa News* reported that the boys were "earnest and positive in their conviction" that Vreeland was the man they'd seen. Gordon Wolf, the last member of the ill-fated party, however, said that he couldn't be sure Vreeland was the man he'd seen. Gordon, the boy who was not named in the first few articles concerning the case, said that he was a long way off and did not get a good look at the man from whom he ran.

This was the break investigators had been searching after for so long: positive identification of the man who'd last been seen with Buddy. "The sheriff's office and police regarded it as the most startling development in the investigation," the *Wauwatosa News* noted. Hopes immediately rose that this man was the one who'd committed such a horrible crime and that justice would soon be served.

The district attorney also called in four other boys that day: Paul Schemling, eleven; Roman Krueger, nine; Clarence Butin, fourteen; and Lawrence Nelson, ten. None of the boys said that he had been molested by Vreeland or could identify him.

The *Milwaukee Sentinel*, in its usually sensationalistic manner of the day, got together with the local authorities to set up some photographs that no respectable newspaper or law enforcement agency would agree to setting up today. On September 16, the *Sentinel* published a photo of Buddy's companions seated in chairs at the district attorney's office facing Vreeland, sitting so close to the man they said they suspected of killing their friend that one of the boy's feet was nearly touching Vreeland's. The boys each had an arm outstretched, pointing at Vreeland, and a white dashed arrow was drawn going from their fingertips to Vreeland's chest, the accused sitting calmly with his hands clasped together in his lap.

A head/shoulders shot of Vreeland accompanied that photo, his hair slicked back and his eyes open wide, staring eerily intently at the camera. His left eyelid drooped slightly, as if he had a lazy eye.

In the following day's paper, the *Sentinel* published a series of three photographs side by side. The first showed six Wauwatosa boys standing within a couple feet of Vreeland at the district attorney's office. Vreeland looked down at the boys past his long nose with his hands in his coat pockets. The second photograph showed two of the boys, Arnold Yunk and John Wolf, standing beside a desk in the district attorney's office, with Vreeland sitting at one side of the desk and a member of the DA's staff at the other side. The third

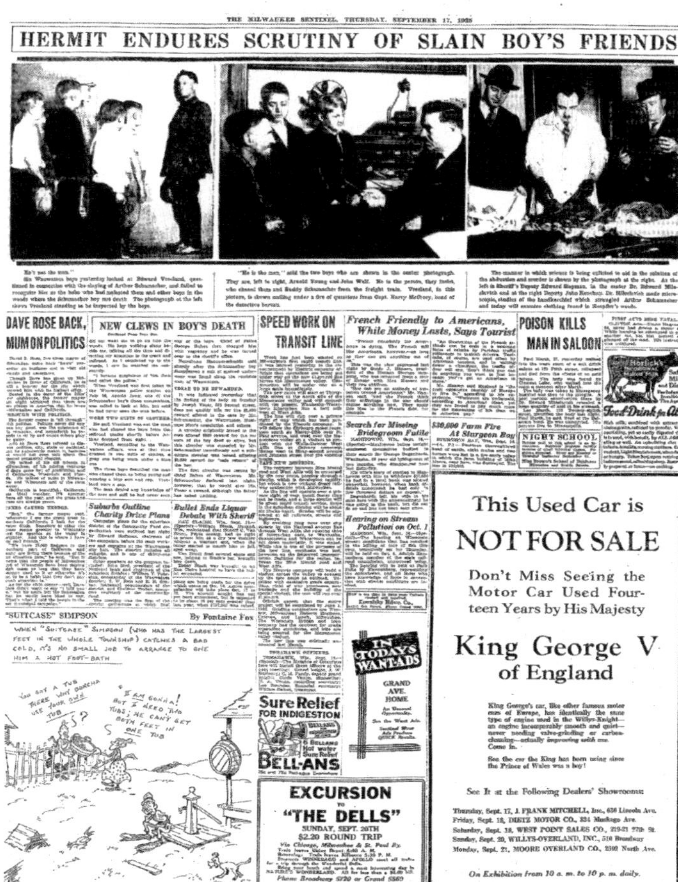

THE MILWAUKEE SENTINEL, THURSDAY, SEPTEMBER 17, 1925

HERMIT ENDURES SCRUTINY OF SLAIN BOY'S FRIENDS

DAVE ROSE BACK, MUM ON POLITICS

NEW CLEWS IN BOY'S DEATH

SPEED WORK ON TRANSIT LINE

French Friendly to Americans, While Money Lasts, Says Tourist

POISON KILLS MAN IN SALOON

"SUITCASE" SIMPSON — By Fontaine Fox

This Used Car is NOT FOR SALE

Don't Miss Seeing the Motor Car Used Fourteen Years by His Majesty

King George V of England

Sure Relief FOR INDIGESTION — BELL-ANS

EXCURSION TO "THE DELLS" SUNDAY, SEPT. 20TH $2.20 ROUND TRIP — Dells Boat Company

"Hermit Endures Scrutiny of Slain Boy's Friends" *Milwaukee Sentinel*, September 17, 1925.

photo showed three men examining Buddy's clothing and the handkerchief that was used to kill him. The headline above the three photos read, "Hermit Endures Scrutiny Of Slain Boy's Friends." The text under the photos read:

> *"He's not the man." Six Wauwatosa boys yesterday looked at Edward Vreeland, questioned in connection with the slaying of Arthur Schumacher, and failed to recognize him as the hobo who had molested them and other boys in the woods where the Schumacher boy met death. "He is the man," said the two boys who are shown in the center photograph. They are, left to right, Arnold Young and John Wolf. He is the person, they insist, who chased them and Buddy Schumacher from the freight train. Vreeland, in this picture, is shown smiling under a fire of questions from Capt. Harry McCrory, head of the detective bureau. The manner in which science is being enlisted to aid in the solution of the abduction and murder is shown by the photograph at the right. At the left is Sheriff's Deputy Edward Siepman. In the center Dr. Edward Miloslavich who made microscopic studies of the handkerchief which strangled Arthur Schumacher and today will examine clothing found in Koepfler's woods.*

The story that accompanied these photos in the September 17 *Milwaukee Sentinel* revealed some new facts. First of all, two prisoners at the house of corrections asked to see Deputies Siepman and Lenehan. After their conversation, the deputies "left hastily, apparently to follow a lead suggested by the prisoners." The deputies stayed out all night. But when morning arrived, their superiors knew nothing of any new developments.

However, there was another most interesting development that day: the finding of a blue coat at the county jail. A note attached to the coat alleged that it was left there by Vreeland when he left for the house of correction. The man who chased Buddy Schumacher and his companions from the train was said to have been wearing two coats at the time, one light and one dark, according to the boys. Vreeland was wearing a tan coat at the house of correction at this time.

Vreeland, according to Wauwatosa police, was wearing two suits of clothes at the time that Buddy vanished—a gray one underneath a blue one—and he also wore a cap. Meanwhile, the boys who were with Buddy said that the man who chased them was young, wore a blue suit and a cap. In addition to the discovery of the blue coat, authorities also discovered underwear and other clothing in Koepfler's woods. None of this clothing appeared to belong to Buddy, though.

Once again, the *Milwaukee Journal* took a more reserved route with its coverage of Vreeland being identified by the boys. A two-column headline simply stated, "VAGRANT IS IDENTIFIED BY SLAIN BOY'S PALS" in the September 16 editions. A one-column photo of Vreeland standing in the Wauwatosa Police Department accompanied the story.

Among the revelations in this story was the report of a nineteen-year-old Wauwatosa man stating that he'd seen a "tramp" on the riverbank near Koepfler's woods shortly before Buddy went missing. Harry Sellhausen had been camping west of Wauwatosa and went to the river for water. He told police that he was approached by a tramp and saw the man several times.

"He acted queerly," Sellhausen said, "and after that, I carried a hatchet to the river." He also said that he saw a handkerchief in the man's possession and believed that he could recognize that handkerchief if he were to see it again. There was no mention in succeeding papers whether Sellhausen was shown a photo of the handkerchief found in Buddy's throat or not.

A September 17 *Journal* story detailed the accounts of three more witnesses, adding their weight to the testimony against Vreeland. Two

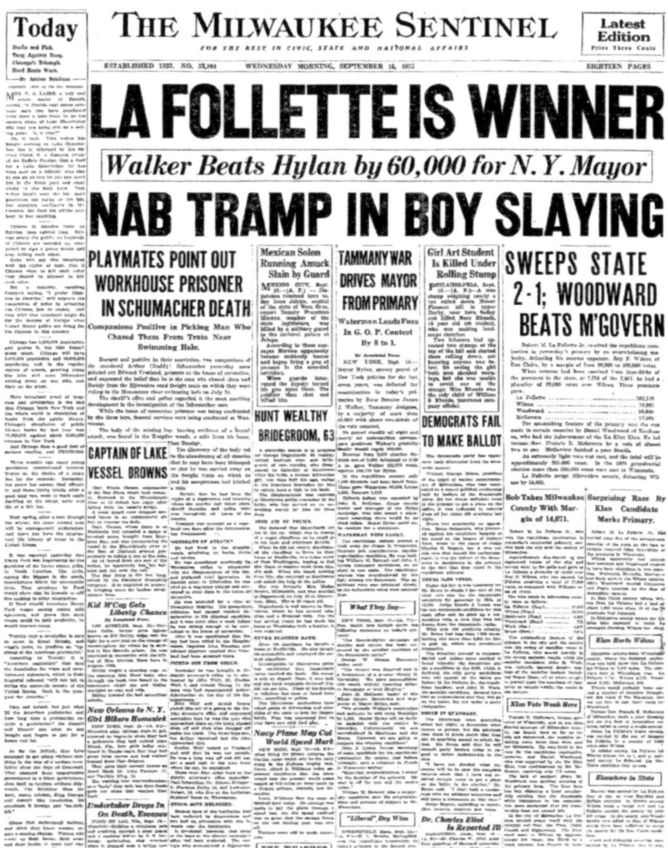

Today

THE MILWAUKEE SENTINEL

Latest Edition

WEDNESDAY MORNING, SEPTEMBER 16, 1925

EIGHTEEN PAGES

LA FOLLETTE IS WINNER

Walker Beats Hylan by 60,000 for N. Y. Mayor

NAB TRAMP IN BOY SLAYING

PLAYMATES POINT OUT WORKHOUSE PRISONER IN SCHUMACHER DEATH

Companions Positive in Picking Man Who Chased Them From Train Near Swimming Hole.

Mexican Solon Running Amuck Slain by Guard

TAMMANY WAR DRIVES MAYOR FROM PRIMARY

Waterman Leads Foes In G. O. P. Contest By 8 to 1.

Girl Art Student Is Killed Under Rolling Stump

SWEEPS STATE 2-1; WOODWARD BEATS M'GOVERN

HUNT WEALTHY BRIDEGROOM, 63

CAPTAIN OF LAKE VESSEL DROWNS

DEMOCRATS FAIL TO MAKE BALLOT

Bob Takes Milwaukee County With Margin of 14,671.

Surprising Race By Klan Candidate Marks Primary.

"Nab Tramp in Boy Slaying," *Milwaukee Sentinel*, September 16, 1925.

of the witnesses were ten-year-old boys who said that Vreeland had taken them for a walk through the grounds of the hospital for mental diseases and "mistreated them." Vreeland, when confronted with the boys, recognized them but denied mistreating them. "I have seen them before," Vreeland said. "In fact, I have talked with them in the woods, I believe, but what they say is not true. I never did such things."

The third new witness, according to the article, was Arthur Haase, who was four months into a two-year sentence for forgery in the local house of correction. He had applied for parole several days before he was taken to the district attorney's office on September 17 and was questioned by District Attorney Wengert and George Bowman, Wengert's assistant. Haase said that he'd spoken with Vreeland while both were serving time.

"I was in the smoking room at the house of correction," Haase told the authorities. "Vreeland came up and said I looked like a man he could trust. Then, he asked about the Schumacher case and asked if I knew how much reward was offered for discovery of the boy. He said when the reward got big enough he would go out and look. He said he knew all about the country around where the boy disappeared." Haase went on to say that Vreeland had told him that he'd been with Buddy the day Buddy disappeared. "He said he knew the boy and gave him some frog legs that morning," Haase said.

Vreeland was questioned regarding Haase's assertions, first alone and then with Haase present. Vreeland denied saying any such things and said that he'd never even talked to Haase at all.

Three other prisoners at the house of correction were questioned on September 17 regarding Vreeland. Thomas Conway, Joseph Klatt and John Nowakowski had worked beside Vreeland there since August, and all told Wengert that Vreeland spoke of the Schumacher case with "extreme apprehension," according to a September 18 *Sentinel* story. Vreeland, the prisoners said, many times gave them reason to suspect that he thought he'd be charged with more crimes than just vagrancy. However, they said that "he was not specific in discussing what was preying on his mind."

Vreeland continued to be questioned each day, but nothing much was gained from it, and he was returned to the house of correction on September 18. Wengert couldn't find anything else to hold him on, but since he was still nearby, he could be called to the police station again at a moment's notice. Meanwhile, Miloslavich said that there were no marks on the handkerchief that could connect it to Vreeland.

"The case is up against a stone wall," Wengert said. "We know little more than we did the day the boy's body was discovered."

Chapter 13

SUSPECT LINKED TO MURDER WEAPON

Just one day after sending Edward Vreeland back to the house of correction, the district attorney summoned him back to the Wauwatosa police station for further questioning. Apparently, several people pointed out flaws in Vreeland's life story to investigators, especially concerning his testimony of his time in Koepfler's woods. That sparked authorities to launch a line of questioning designed to uncover every minute detail of Vreeland's life, his habits and, particularly, his residence in the woods where the body was found.

Authorities again became interested in Frank Blue, the railroad employee who had said that he'd seen some boys and a man on the train as it passed by him the day Buddy disappeared. It was determined that Blue was in Chicago, and he was to be summoned to see if he could identify Vreeland.

Meanwhile, the eyewitness accounts of John Wolf and Arnold Yunk had been seen as being weakened a bit. A couple days after Buddy was buried, they now recalled that the man they'd seen with him had a mustache; Vreeland did not. However, the boys still said that he looked like the man even without a mustache. Authorities also finally recalled that Yunk, just two days after his friend had disappeared, had said at that time that Vreeland was not the man who chased them from the train.

Vreeland, meanwhile, said that while he was camping just west of Wauwatosa he'd seen a patient from the county hospital for mental diseases roaming that area. This man had a mustache, Vreeland asserted, and more closely matched the boys' description than did he. Vreeland reportedly had answered all questions "in a straightforward manner and without hesitancy." He continued to steadfastly deny that he ever saw any of the boys before they confronted him at the police station or that he knew anything about the death of Buddy Schumacher.

The developments left the district attorney with less hope of bringing Vreeland to trial. "What we have learned about this man is not enough to charge him with any serious offense," Wengert said on September 18. "If our alternative was to turn him loose we might have to take a chance on a warrant. As it is, however, he has some 15 days to serve and during that time we can continue to investigate."

Three days later, Vreeland was back at the county jail for further questioning to discuss accusations that he lured a fifteen-year-old Milwaukee boy into the woods and attempted to molest him near where Buddy was found. Fred Stubbe said that Vreeland had carried an improvised fishing pole and a basket at the time.

When confronted with Stubbe's story, Vreeland said that the boy's face looked familiar, but he denied any wrongdoing. However, Vreeland, who was said to be deeply religious and would not go to sleep unless a Bible were placed under his pillow, admitted the next day that Stubbe's story was indeed correct after spending several hours reading his Bible. After a few days of questioning, though, Vreeland had not confessed to Buddy's slaying, saying that he didn't remember anything of the Schumacher boy.

Vreeland finally told Wengert that he had been kicked in the head by a horse many years ago and that he sometimes suffered from "queer spells" and memory lapses after which he had no recollection of what he'd done. Vreeland said that he sometimes would awaken to find himself "raving at night" and then be unable to resume sleep. The disease was described by psychologists as a form of aphasia, a class of language disorders that range from having difficulty remembering words to being completely unable to speak, read or write. Aphasia disorders usually develop quickly as a result of head injury or stroke or slowly from a brain tumor, infection or dementia, or they can be a learning disability.

Vreeland still denied being aware of the Schumacher boy. "If I have done anything wrong," Edward Vreeland said in a September 22 *Milwaukee Sentinel* report, "it was certainly during such a spell, for I know nothing about it." This disclosure did revive the inquiry into his possible involvement in the Schumacher case.

The following day, a "crippled" inmate of one of the county institutions was picked up by Wauwatosa police in the woods west of Wauwatosa, where he and other men, presumably hoboes, had a sort of camp. Three Wauwatosa boys identified the man as one who guarded the camp while the others foraged for handouts. The man denied having any hobo friends and said that he knew nothing of any man named Vreeland. In the camp, however, authorities found newspapers with stories of the discovery of the Schumacher boy's body and the questioning of Vreeland.

Edward Vreeland's brother, Charles Vreeland, arrived from Davenport, Iowa (or Peoria, Illinois, as he was reported to be from both cities), about the time Edward discussed his blackouts, and Charles retained attorney Louis Koenig to represent his brother. Charles Vreeland told the assistant district attorney that he was "anxious" to keep the news of his brother's charges quiet from their mother, an eighty-three-year-old woman living in Lockport, Illinois.

Through questioning of Vreeland and his brother, it was learned that Edward Vreeland had been married twice and was a father of four children, the oldest being a fifteen-year-old girl. Vreeland said that his second wife had left him. Grandfathers on both sides of his family had been ministers, and Vreeland had also been a student of religion.

After the final questioning on the night of September 21, Vreeland said that he had something important to say to his brother the next day, giving his jailers hope that a confession was forthcoming. There was no confession the next day, but developments described as being of "utmost importance" followed additional questioning of Vreeland on September 22. This questioning was done mainly by Kroening and concerned Vreeland's account of his activities while he lived in the Koepfler woods. This additional information was gathered in the presence of Vreeland's brother, as well as Deputies Siepman and Kenehan.

The difficulty in getting Vreeland to either remember or admit to what everyone suspected he'd done to Buddy caused local authorities to try something unique. Since Vreeland was quite religious, an evangelist was asked to come and "probe the soul" of the suspect, according to Kroening. The request was called "startling and revolutionary in crime detection" in a United Press story.

The story went on to say that deputies "have thrust a Bible into Vreeland's hands, and he has perused the testament fervidly." Authorities hoped that if Vreeland was, in fact, guilty he would "break down under the stress of a religious frenzy, and perhaps free a tormented conscience of a loathsome secret." If no confession is obtained, the evangelist was to be brought in to pray with him. Authorities believed that if Vreeland did commit the murder, he would admit it in a "sawdust trail" confession. (The term "sawdust trail" came from the sawdust-covered aisles in the temporary constructions put up for revival meetings in early twentieth-century America. That type of confession was seen as one made on the road to conversion or rehabilitation. It was said that legal criminologists were eagerly awaiting the results of this latest "third degree" method.)

One of the best pieces of evidence pointing to Vreeland as Buddy's killer came to light on September 24 as an apparent connection was made between him and the handkerchief found in the boy's throat. Emma Abel, known in all the newspaper reports of the time only as Mrs. George Abel, lived near Koepfler's woods south of North Avenue on Lovers Lane Road (now Mayfair Road) and told authorities that she'd seen Vreeland with a similar handkerchief, including the letter "A" stitched in the corner, when Vreeland came to her home for food a few days before Buddy's disappearance. Why it took Emma Abel a week to tell authorities that she'd seen a man with what may have been the implement of Buddy's murder is a question that was never answered.

A photo of Mrs. Abel was shown on the front page of the next day's *Milwaukee Sentinel* with a pen and paper, "as she drew from memory the initial she said she saw" in Vreeland's hands. Vreeland was said to be unshaken by this development.

The *Milwaukee Sentinel* provided a very detailed account of the circumstances surrounding Mrs. Abel's meetings with Vreeland and how she came in contact with his initialed handkerchief. In the *Journal* story of September 24, Mrs. Abel said that she knew Vreeland because he had come to her home many times to beg for food. She said that she had taken pity on him and supplied him with food. She also said she had seen Vreeland with a handkerchief with the initial "A" on it.

Deputies asked her to come to the district attorney's office to identify the handkerchief. But since the handkerchief could not immediately be found, she went back home, where she lived with her husband and three children. She was reached by a *Journal* reporter at home and was asked to describe the handkerchief that Vreeland had carried. A *Journal* photographer had taken a photo of the handkerchief after it has been cleaned, and the reporter had the photo in front of him when he made the call to the Abel residence.

"How does it happen, Mrs. Abel, that you are able to recall distinctly such a minor thing as a man's handkerchief?" she was asked by the reporter.

"Well, he showed it to me and we talked about how dirty it was," she explained. "You see, he came to the door about a week before the Schumacher boy disappeared. He had been there before to get food. It was a warm day and he pulled the handkerchief from his upper coat pocket and wiped his face with it. 'I guess I ought to wash this handkerchief,' he said to me. 'It's pretty dirty.' Yes, I said. You certainly should…He asked for a bar of soap so he could wash it and I went to get the soap. When I came back, he was wiping his neck with the handkerchief. He spread it out and looked at it and said 'Oh, I guess I'll wait a while till it gets dirtier and then wash it.'"

The reporter asked Emma Abel if she'd seen any initial on it.

"Oh yes, there was a letter A in one corner."

"How large was it?"

"Medium large, I should say," she replied.

The photo was said to have displayed a fairly large letter A in a corner of the handkerchief. The reporter continued with his questioning.

"Was it plain or fancy?"

"It seemed to be embroidered in silk and there were some fancy ends and something on the side," she said.

The reporter checked the photo again. There were flowered ends on the initial and a sort of flower on the side.

"What sort of cross piece did the letter have?" Mrs. Abel was asked.

"It bent in the middle."

"How do you mean? Up or down?"

"It bent so when it joined the sides it made a sort of diamond shape," she said.

The photograph showed that the cross piece of the A bent downward, making an irregular diamond shape with the juncture of the two sides.

"Are you sure you remember the letter distinctly, Mrs. Abel?" the reporter asked.

"Oh yes, I think I could draw it."

A reporter was sent to Mrs. Abel's home, and she drew the letter for him as she remembered it. The sketch was reported to match up fairly well with the photo. The picture was then finally shown to Mrs. Abel, who said that it was indeed a photo of the handkerchief she'd seen in Vreeland's hands.

Meanwhile, Vreeland was taken to the site where Buddy's body was found to see if that might jog his memory. But Vreeland again said that he had no knowledge of the disappearance or killing. A United Press story of September 25 reported that Vreeland, "standing near the clump of bushes in which Arthur's body was found took off his hat and dramatically declared 'Before God I am innocent.'"

The *Milwaukee Sentinel*'s version of the story noted that "[s]urrounded by sheriff's deputies, detectives and newspaper men in a little group that stood in Koepfler's woods yesterday, Edward Vreeland took off his cap, while a forest breeze tousled his hair, asserted solemnly that he knew nothing of the disappearance and slaying of Arthur Schumacher."

While at the spot where the body was found, it was reported that Vreeland manifested some amount of curiosity, as did the rest of the group. He watched attentively while it was explained that the body was hidden by this particular bush, that the head lay here and the feet lay there. Then, "deeply affected, he turned away and made his declaration of innocence." It was said that Vreeland dramatically and without prompting from any of the officers about him made his oath. "Before God I am innocent," he said solemnly. "Or," he added, "if I had anything to do with it, I was out of my mind at the time and I don't remember now."

Police weren't convinced.

Chapter 14

THE CASE SUDDENLY FALLS APART

As the religious fervor angle failed to produce a confession, authorities were prepared to turn to science, contemplating administering a truth serum to Vreeland. The exact type of truth serum was not mentioned, and it's not certain if authorities actually went ahead with this plan. Had they used it, it would have been pretty cutting edge for an investigation in the 1920s.

It was only about ten years earlier that a rural Texas obstetrician by the name of Dr. Robert House noticed that the popular obstetric anesthetic drug scopolamine, also known as twilight sleep, would put his patients into a state where they would deliver information in a way that seemed automatic, noted an article in the December 4, 2008 issue of *Scientific American*.

Some time later, drugs such as scopolamine got a reputation for having the power to force people to provide information against their will. It is thought that some U.S. police agencies were using these drugs for this purpose by sometime in the 1920s. Later investigations proved this to be true but also that there was not a lot of documentation of these practices.

Today, the idea that a drug can reliably extract information that one does not wish to share isn't widely accepted, the article noted. Ever since the 1920s, many judges, psychiatrists and scientists have rejected this idea. They have said, however, that certain drugs may make people feel more like talking. But it also puts them in a state of extreme suggestibility, where people under the influence of these types of drugs will pick up on cues about what the questioners want to hear and repeat that back.

Back in the mid-1920s, however, the fascination with the potential that truth serums held may have been enough for authorities to try in a case such as the Schumacher murder. But considering that police had eyewitness accounts tying Edward Vreeland to Buddy the day the boy disappeared, had a connection between Vreeland and the handkerchief used to kill the boy and also had Vreeland tied to the site where the body was found, this case seemed to be coming to a conclusion. Wauwatosa was sure that it had its man.

But soon the case against Edward Vreeland fell apart one piece after another, and it did so in some quite peculiar ways. First, the handkerchief and Buddy's clothing were unable to be located at the district attorney's office for a few days. This was discovered when Mrs. Abel went to the office to identify the handkerchief in person. When she got there, the only real material clue in the case was gone.

District Attorney Wengert admitted that he had received the items from the sheriff's office. But a thorough search of his office failed to locate them. They were found a few days later in Wengert's safe, where they had been placed "unbeknown to officials," according to a story in the October 1 *Wauwatosa News*.

The Milwaukee County sheriff's office and the district attorney's office fired barbs at each other over the handkerchief's disappearance, each accusing the other of misdeeds. The September 25 *Milwaukee Sentinel* reported that Undersheriff Kroening wrote to the county board complaining that the DA and his staff had not cooperated with the sheriff's department on the Schumacher case. When informed of Kroening's letter, District Attorney Wengert replied, "I hope the county board does investigate. Then I'll ask a few pointed questions of the sheriff's department myself. I'll inquire about certain leaks in the sheriff's department." Wengert would not elaborate on the nature of these leaks when asked by a *Journal* reporter, but he said that the sheriff and his chief aides would know well enough what was meant.

The handkerchief found in Buddy's throat had been on Wengert's desk. But it could not be found when Kroening went to Wengert's office to look for it on Thursday morning, September 24. Wengert then ordered his staff to search diligently for the handkerchief. He alleged that the sheriff's department may have taken it. This was denied by Kroening.

Peeved at what he termed a "lack of interest and cooperation of the district attorney and his staff," climaxing in the disappearance of Exhibit A (the handkerchief), Kroening called in a stenographer and dictated the following letter to the Milwaukee County Board:

To the Chairman of the County Board:

Dear Sir—I feel it is my duty to call attention to the fact that through the apparent carelessness of the district attorney's office the most important bit of evidence in the murder of Arthur Schumacher has been mislaid. That is the handkerchief which was wadded in the boy's throat by the person who committed the crime.

As a result the investigation carried on by the sheriff's office has been seriously hampered. We have a suspect under arrest. Edward Vreeland, who has been identified by a woman, Mrs. George Abel, as the owner of the handkerchief. Mrs. Abel, Thursday, even went so far as to recognize the handkerchief as Vreeland's from a picture taken by the Milwaukee Sentinel. *Loss of the greatest evidence, the handkerchief, will make it difficult to substantiate our claim.*

In conclusion, I take the privilege of informing your body that the handkerchief, if it is lost, is the direct result of carelessness by the district attorney's office. The sheriff's office has not received the slightest cooperation in any effort it has made to bring the crime to a solution.

Instead, there have been noticeable attempts to block us at every opportunity. This I am prepared to substantiate by Siepman and Kenehan, who have worked on the case. Upon the receipt of this letter it is the hope of the sheriff's department that a thorough investigation be undertaken by the county board to learn why the handkerchief, found in the murdered boy's body, should disappear at so vital a time.

Respectfully,
Herman Kroening
Undersheriff

How in the world does the only piece of hard evidence in a murder investigation, especially in such a high-profile case as this one, get lost? Either way, Wengert apparently found the handkerchief a day or two later. Wengert said that he found it in his safe on either September 25 or 26 (the *Journal* story reporting this gave two different days). He said that the handkerchief, wrapped in paper, was lying on his desk one day with several other packages when he was called away. He told a clerk to put all the packages in the safe, and that was done. Wengert said that he had no idea that the handkerchief had been placed in the safe with the other packages. He finally opened every package in the safe and found the handkerchief.

Meanwhile, Wengert shot back at Kroening's accusations as he spoke to a *Journal* reporter. Wengert said that Kroening "went off half cocked" in writing a letter to the county board. Kroening also took offense to Wengert's assertion that there were leaks in the sheriff's department. "Wengert is talking through his hat. There are no leaks here unless the gas pipes are leaking," Kroening said. "We have nothing to fear from an investigation."

Now that the handkerchief was located, all that had to be done was bring it to Mrs. Abel and have her identify it in person. That would seem to be enough evidence to charge Vreeland with Buddy's murder. But when the handkerchief was presented to her, she said that she could not positively identify it as the one she'd considered washing for Vreeland. While she admitted that the initial "A" looked like the initial she'd seen, she said that she could not be certain that this handkerchief was the same one she'd seen in Vreeland's hands.

What just happened here? The handkerchief was identified from a photo, but when seen in person a few days later, after said handkerchief had been missing for a few days, it cannot be positively identified? Was Mrs. Abel simply wrong when she saw the photo? Did someone switch out evidence, taking the handkerchief that killed Buddy Schumacher and replacing it with another, similar handkerchief? Did someone get to Mrs. Abel and convince her to change her story? If so, why? Or did she not tell the truth to begin with and was now coming clean?

These are questions that may never be answered, but the fact that the handkerchief could no longer be connected to Vreeland left only eyewitness accounts linking the "hobo" to the young boy. And if the only evidence against him was that he had been seen with Buddy, even that might not be enough to bring him to trial.

The *Milwaukee Sentinel*, in its September 27 edition, noted, "Complete collapse of the investigation of the murder of Arthur (Buddy) Schumacher, Wauwatosa, was seen yesterday when Mrs. George Abel failed to identify the handkerchief used to gag the young boy as the one she saw in the hands of Edward Vreeland, the hermit, who has withstood the grilling of the police and sheriff's deputies for almost two weeks."

District Attorney Wengert agreed, saying in a September 25 *Milwaukee Sentinel* story that there wasn't enough evidence to charge Edward Vreeland with murder and indicated that he would not issue such a warrant. "If the sheriff's department asks a warrant charging the man with misconduct to minors, I may agree to a charge of that kind," Wengert stated. But not one of murder.

That last week of September brought allegations of cruel treatment to Vreeland, sparking his attorney to attempt to have his client served with a writ of habeus corpus, which allows prisoners to be released from unlawful detention.

While Vreeland was being held at the sheriff's office undergoing questioning, deputy sheriffs and jailers were tipped off that Vreeland's attorney was about to serve the writ. Vreeland was then hustled into an automobile and hurried back to the house of correction, where he was serving the vagrancy sentence. Authorities beat the writ by ten minutes, according to the September 26 *Milwaukee Sentinel*. Two hours later, Deputy Sheriffs August C. Hageman and Thomas C. Traeumer, as well as Assistant District Attorney George Bowman, appeared before circuit court commissioner R.J. Hennessey testifying that Vreeland had been removed from their custody before the writ had been served.

In the writ, Vreeland's brother, Charles, charged that local authorities were persecuting Edward despite his brother having cooperated fully with investigators for a week at the sheriff's office. It was during this time that Charles Vreeland said that he had become convinced that his brother was innocent of killing Buddy Schumacher.

The *Sentinel*'s story noted that "the writ charged that Vreeland has been subjected constantly to 'cruel and inhuman treatment' in efforts of deputy sheriffs to wring a confession from him, in spite of the fact that the man has responded to all questioning freely. It was also charged that continuation of such tactics would cause danger of a forced confession from the man in spite of his protestations of innocence and the absence of any evidence against him."

Even though the writ didn't free Vreeland, the threat of it did move him back to his jail cell and away from the sheriff's department. Meanwhile, the case against him continued to deteriorate. All of a sudden, Buddy's companions reported that they no longer thought Vreeland was the man who chased them from the train.

How could these boys go from being so certain that Vreeland was the man they had seen with their friend to being pretty sure that he was not that man over a period of about two weeks? Were they pressured or "guided" into picking Vreeland out of the police lineup in the first place and were now telling the truth? Did they ever really think that this was their friend's killer and just went along with what everyone was saying or wanted to be true? After all, the whole town was sure that police had the man who killed Buddy Schumacher. Or had the youngsters been asked or told to change their story for some reason?

With the only compelling evidence to try Vreeland for Buddy's murder drying up, police were forced to let him go on October 2, when his vagrancy term had concluded.

Chapter 15

A CONFESSION

It's not known what happened to Edward Vreeland after he was let go, although his brother, Charles, most likely took him out of state. An Ancestry.com family tree lists an Edward Vreeland as dying on February 17, 1938, at fifty-eight years of age in an unknown location. The age matches up with how old Vreeland would have been.

Having to let Vreeland go free must have shocked and infuriated the Wauwatosa community. Countless people had searched and prayed. Parents had been worried for their own children's safety and had kept a much tighter leash on them after the disappearance, especially in the Schumacher household.

Even decades later, the Menomonee River was made strictly off-limits by Buddy's sister, Jeanette (Schumacher) Egloff, to her sons, Brian and Gerald Egloff, who lived with Art and Florence during World War II while Jeanette's husband, Lee, was away on military duty. "When we were young boys, we knew that Mother's brother had been murdered. We were sternly warned not to worry Grandmother and not to play by the river," Brian Egloff said. "Which we did, but once got caught by the police, and Mom spanked us."

When Vreeland was released, many local residents—and probably the local law enforcement community as well—thought that they were watching a guilty man skip town without justice being served. Anyone who knew anything about the case knew that evidence had gone missing and witnesses had changed their stories. One can only imagine what John and Gordon Wolf and Arnold Yunk went through, with inquisitive classmates and others curious as to why the boys had changed their tunes.

Meanwhile, police and sheriff's offices had to go about business with the attitude that Buddy's killer was still at large, whether they believed it or not. However, there was little or nothing to go on at this point. Authorities needed a big break.

They thought that they got that break in the middle of October when the warden at a prison in Stillwater, Minnesota, summoned Milwaukee police detective Adolph Kraemer to question a man who had just been convicted of killing an eleven-year-old boy in St. Paul. William Brandt, a twenty-one-year-old former Milwaukee newspaper delivery boy with some mental deficiencies, had just been charged with murder in the death of Francis Pioletti. The warden had noticed some similarities between the Pioletti and Schumacher murders, including the fact that both victims had been gagged with handkerchiefs, causing him to call Milwaukee.

According to an Associated Press story in the *New York Times*, Brandt had lured Pioletti from play with the promise of employment as a distributor of samples. Police determined that Brandt had beaten the boy to death with a gas pipe during a violent struggle in the basement of a vacant house and then carried the body to the attic, where the body was found in a dark corner. When the boy didn't return home that evening, a police search turned up the body. Not long afterward, they found Brandt hiding under a bed in his home. After two hours of questioning, Brandt confessed to the Pioletti killing.

Brandt, who also went by the alias "William Spaz," was described in a United Press story as slender and gaunt. He seemed to match the description of the mysterious man on the train given by Buddy's companions, and he'd also been linked to more attacks on small boys in the Twin Cities area.

Milwaukee detectives who questioned Brandt on November 8 were sure that they had Buddy's killer. Brandt was cross-examined by Kraemer at length and admitted that he was in Milwaukee around the time Buddy disappeared. Later, Brandt denied this and, after further questioning, collapsed in his cell. Kraemer returned to Milwaukee to check up on Brandt's story about his residence in Milwaukee that summer. At the time, police said that Brandt's denials of the Schumacher crime were more like rambling explanations and that they were satisfied that he had something on his mind that he wasn't sharing.

Physicians said that Brandt's "mentality was high for a moron and said he was capable of standing trial for murder," a story in the November 9 *Waukesha Freeman* noted. In another story, Brandt was described by "alienists," or psychiatrists, as having the mind of someone ten years and eight months old but that he was not insane. He pleaded not guilty at his arraignment to the Pioletti slaying, even though he'd previously confessed. Eventually, he was sentenced to life in prison for the murder, called by St. Paul police "one of the most dastardly crimes in Minnesota history."

Brandt didn't give police enough to go on in order to pursue further investigation of him in connection with Buddy. With Brandt seemingly out of the mix as a suspect, the case came to a standstill once again. Less than two weeks later, however, Brandt stunned authorities by confessing to the murder of Buddy Schumacher. The United Press story that appeared in the *Waukesha Daily Freeman* on November 24 pegged the exact hour of Brandt's confession at 11:00 a.m. that day.

Reports of the circumstances surrounding the confession differed. In a United Press report that was published in the *Sheboygan Press* on November 25, Brandt's confession to officers at the Stillwater prison was characterized as being done in quite a calm manner and volunteered. According to the story, Brandt had "acted queerly" for several days and had several times asked to see the warden, J.J. Sullivan. But each time the warden would go to his cell, Brandt would refuse to talk. Finally, Brandt started talking. He said that he didn't remember anything of the crime itself but remembered being with Buddy shortly before he lost consciousness, and when he regained consciousness, he saw the boy's body lying next to him.

"I guess I killed that boy in Milwaukee," Brandt was quoted as saying. "I do not remember killing him. But I remember being with him and I remember hiding the body."

The *Milwaukee Sentinel*'s account in its November 24 Final Edition was similar to the United Press story. It noted that Brandt's confession was volunteered to the warden. The warden thought that Brandt's claim of memory loss could be true, as Brandt had spells of unconsciousness several times in prison since his arrest.

The *Wauwatosa News*' account of the Brandt confession painted a much different picture, however. The Schumachers' hometown newspaper reported the confession came while Brandt was being questioned about his movements before the Pioletti murder. When Brandt was pressed for details on his whereabouts during July, he said that he had been working in the harvest fields of the Dakotas during the time Buddy disappeared. But there was no harvesting in the Dakotas in July.

After trapping himself in this lie, Brandt further entangled himself in more lies, according to the story. Finally, he became flustered and shouted, "I killed the Wauwatosa boy. I am here for life anyway. Why should I hide it?" At that point, according to the article, Brandt made a full confession. His alleged confession was printed in great detail in a *Journal* article:

> *I was riding through Wauwatosa on July 24, 1925, in a box car when I noticed a bunch of boys, and all run away except one. He was Arthur Schumacher. I got off the box car and asked the boy why the rest of the boys disappeared. Arthur told me they were afraid of me.*
>
> *I had some liquor in my hip pocket, and the young fellow noticed it and told me to hide it. I stood for a while talking to the boy and he finally started off, and I asked him to wait a while. We walked to some bushes and there met another man about 45 years old, who had some denatured alcohol.*
>
> *I asked this man what he was doing there, and he replied he was bumming a few drinks of each kind of liquor.*
>
> *I started smoking a cigarette and Arthur asked me for one. I told him smoking would make him sick, and at first refused to give the boy any. Later on I gave the boy a cigarette and that's all I remember. Arthur was sitting near me on the ground, until I came to, and found myself hugging and chocking* [sic] *the boy.*
>
> *I admit I had him in the same way as the Pioletti boy, in St. Paul. When I looked at him then he was dead. I noticed his clothes were covered in blood and his body cut in many places.*
>
> *I don't remember how this was done, but noticed an old tin can near the body which I think I used in cutting the boy. I took off the boy's overalls and stuffed them in a drain pipe which was a short distance from the railroad tracks.*
>
> *I then took a clean handkerchief which I had with me, tore off my initials and stuffed the handkerchief in his mouth. I threw the body in the bushes.*
>
> *I went to North Dakota from Milwaukee and went from there to St. Paul. The boys in Wisconsin who were with us just prior to this were expected to come to St. Paul to identify me, but did not come.*

A United Press report that appeared in the *Waukesha Daily Freeman* the same day added that physicians appointed by the State of Minnesota who examined him stated he was capable of standing trial, even though he was a "10 year old minded moron." But doctors said that he was "high in the scale of moron intelligence," which in their minds was enough to go to trial. The story also noted that when Brandt was arrested in the Pioletti case, "he fought ferociously but broke down under police grilling. In the city jail he became a cringing young animal, frightened almost into hysterics by any untoward sound."

No matter how the confession came about, authorities investigating the Buddy Schumacher case finally had one. You'd think that would have tied up the case. But just as most every other development in this investigation eventually fell apart, so did this one.

Additional questioning by Milwaukee police showed that some details in William Brandt's story didn't match up with the facts of the case:

1. Brandt said that the boy's clothing was covered with blood, whereas officials declared that no blood was found on the clothing when Buddy's body was found.
2. Brandt said that he took off the boy's overalls and stuffed them in a culvert near the railroad tracks, but when Buddy's body was found, the overalls were still on the body.
3. Brandt said that he tore his initials from a handkerchief and stuffed it into Buddy's mouth. The handkerchief found in Buddy's throat was not torn, and the initial "A" was found in one corner.
4. Brandt said that he rolled Buddy over to one side and threw some brush over him. However, when the body was found, there was no brush lying on top of him, nor any loose near him that could have blown off.

Other factors also convinced authorities that Brandt's confession was no good.

Imagine the Schumacher family getting this news. After spending seven excruciating weeks searching and waiting to find out what happened to Buddy, they think that the killer is going to be brought to justice within days of the boy being found. Then the case against that man falls apart. And now, for the second time, they think the boy's killer is in custody. But the man's confession is seen as bogus.

In the Brandt case, authorities determined that he was able to gather enough facts about the case when he was questioned in October to make up a confession in November. Normally, men do not confess to crimes they do not commit. But Brandt was viewed by some psychiatrists as having the type of mental makeup that would lead him to do such a thing, and he perhaps had gained enough knowledge of the Schumacher case to fool authorities into believing his confession…at least momentarily.

Leading further claim to the theory that Brandt did not kill Buddy was the fact that when shown a photograph of Brandt, Buddy's companions were unable to identify him.

"I don't believe I have ever seen him before," John Wolf said. The *Milwaukee Sentinel* published a photo of two of Buddy's pals studying a photo of William Brandt. Information with the photo identified them as John Wolf and Arnold Wolf, but it was most likely John Wolf and Arnold Yunk. At the upper-right corner of this photo was inset a photo of Brandt, and at the lower-left corner was a photo of Buddy.

It was suggested by Stillwater personnel that Brandt's confession may have been some sort of trick. When it was determined that he could not have committed the Schumacher murder, Brandt may have hoped that this would cast doubt on his confession to the Pioletti killing, too.

The day after making his confession, Brandt was questioned again. But he said nothing that couldn't have been picked up from his earlier discussions with Wisconsin law enforcement officials. When he was grilled about the discrepancies in the Schumacher case, Brandt said that he might have been wrong in some of the particulars. He made some rambling explanation of the errors and hid behind his mental ailments, which he said caused him to have "blank spaces" during which he is unable to recall what happens. In an Associated Press report, Brandt said that these "blank spaces" were epileptic fits.

At this same time, authorities finally located the Milwaukee Road worker who said that he saw a man and some boys on a train heading out of Wauwatosa on the morning Buddy went missing. Frank Blue, who had been in Chicago, was sent to Milwaukee for more questions and to view a picture of Brandt. He said that one of the photos of Brandt looked a little like the man he saw that day, but he couldn't make a positive identification.

Stories suggesting that authorities doubted Brandt's confession first appeared in newspapers across Wisconsin and Minnesota on November 25. The *Wauwatosa News* that week, which was not privy to the doubts surrounding Brandt's confession, ran a story announcing that the killer had been captured, with the headline "Murderer Is Caught at Last." The story detailed Brandt's confession and declared the Schumacher case "cleared up." The *News* never ran another story on the Schumacher case.

Chapter 16

WHO WAS WILLIAM BRANDT?

Some details of William Brandt's life are difficult to determine.

His death certificate says that that he was born in 1902. But he seems to be listed in 1900 census records as being born in August 1899. Where he was born is in some question, although several sources point to Illinois. Most sources list he and his older siblings as having been born in Illinois, except in the 1910 census, where they were all listed as having been born in Minnesota.

In three separate census returns, Brandt's father's birthplace was listed as Germany, Illinois and Wisconsin. Brandt's father was listed as being dead in Minnesota prison records but was never named. A family tree posted on Ancestry.com, though, lists Brandt's father as Hubert James Brandt, born in Portage County, Wisconsin, to Prussian immigrants. The 1880 census lists Hubert as a railroad fireman.

Hubert James Brandt's wife was the former Mary Jane Donohue, born in Iowa. This is probably William Brandt's mother, as we know that his mother was named Mary and was born in Iowa, according to several reliable sources.

The couple started their family in Wisconsin in the late 1880s or early 1890s and then moved to Minnesota. By 1900, Mary Brandt was listed as a widow in the census. By that time, she had six children, including nine-month-old William, who may have never known his father.

When he wasn't in a state institution of one sort or another, William Brandt lived most of his young life at 229 Spencer Street in St. Paul. He may have been called Willie as a boy as he was listed under that name in one census report, and he had a middle initial of "E." He was the second youngest of seven children, with four older sisters and an older brother, Hubert J., closest in age to William, not quite four years his senior.

Brandt's mother, listed as Mary Ward on his prison registration form but Mary Brandt in just about all of Brandt's remaining prison records, bore her first three children in Wisconsin and then bore three more in Minnesota following an eight-year gap. It is possible that Mary was married multiple times and that the younger children were fathered by a second husband, who also died or left by the time William was nine months old.

About the time William Brandt was four years old, his mother married Warren Ward, a foreman at a factory in St. Paul. The house William Brandt grew up in could be crowded at times. In the 1900 census, there were six family members, plus five boarders listed as living there, with Mary serving as a housekeeper. According to prison records, William Brandt sometimes used the name William Ward. But sometime between 1910 and 1920, Warren Ward was no longer in the house.

Brandt ran into problems early in life, leaving home at age eight, whereupon he was put into the Parental School and Detention Home in St. Paul, an institution for chronically truant or incorrigible boys. The school and home combination was an intermediate step between regular school and the State Training School at Red Wing, where a child would land after repeated offenses at the school. No doubt his low intelligence had something to do with his problems in school, and he only managed to complete the sixth grade.

Brandt's intelligence was tested three times before he was alleged to have committed the Pioletti murder. Each time, he was judged to have an Intelligence Quotient of between 60 and 63, which classified him as having borderline mental deficiency on the Terman's Stanford-Binet Fourth Revision scale. On the Wechsler Adult Intelligence Scale, those scores put Brandt in the mild mental retardation classification. In these three tests, his "mature age" was never measured higher than nine years, six months.

But prison authorities later said that Brandt seemed to have higher intelligence than this, and the letters he wrote from prison were well thought out and well written, with fairly decent grammar and spelling for someone with just a sixth-grade education.

Brandt also suffered from epileptic seizures, during which his brother said William could become very violent. In fact, shortly after Brandt was incarcerated for the Pioletti murder, Hubert told a story of his brother having pulled a knife on him at home. In a letter from the deputy warden to the warden on December 19, 1925, Hubert related a story that one time when Brandt came home to supper and sat down to the table with his hat on, Hubert ordered him to take it off. When Brandt did not remove the hat, Hubert started to take it off Brandt's head, "and in a flash Brandt drew a knife and swung at his brother cutting through his coat and two shirts."

Hubert warned the deputy sheriff to be careful because Brandt would do anything that came to his mind when he was having one of his epileptic spells and was too dangerous to be allowed to have a job at the prison.

Brandt was first arrested when he was ten years old and was sent to the School for Feeble-Minded and Colony for Epileptics in Fairbault, Minnesota, on May 6, 1913. Brandt hated this place so much that he ran away from it four times over the next five years. This was also the place where Brandt said his sexual desire for young boys was cultivated.

Started in 1879 as an experimental department for "idiotic and feeble-minded children," according to the Minnesota Historical Society, the Fairbault facility's patient population consisted of people of all ages representing all types and degrees of mental retardation, many of whom were also physically infirm.

Brandt detailed the abuse that he said he and his fellow inmates suffered at Fairbault in a long letter dated February 27, 1927. The letter, written from prison about fifteen months after being sentenced for the Pioletti murder, was in response to a request for information of the conditions at the facility, and Brandt said that he wrote it in hopes of relieving other inmates of the suffering he incurred there.

Brandt said that he witnessed many instances of the attendants in Hillcrest House, where he stayed, forcing boys ages eight to fifteen to have sex with them and with one another, as well as commit other unspeakable acts. When an attendant wanted to give one of the boys a beating, he made the boy get undressed and had other boys hold him down while he beat the boy with a rubber hose. If the boys did not do what these attendants told them to do, they'd be beaten and have their lives threatened, according to Brandt, who added that most of the boys were "feeble minded or insane" and could not defend themselves.

If a boy wet or soiled his bed at night, an attendant would rub the boy's face in it, Brandt said. He alleged that one boy's nose started running during an epileptic fit, and the boy was made to lick it off the floor when he came to. The boy was then thrown into a bathtub of cold water, which was something that Brandt said was common to help an epileptic come out of a spell but was not done after he was already out of one. Inmates from the main building would come over sometimes when these boys took showers and snap wet towels at them until they turned black and blue and bled. The attendants looked the other way, he said.

After being there a year, Brandt said that he "got used to the dirty and filthy things they made me do and I did to others what they did to me." He said that he'd never seen such sexually perverse behavior before he got to Fairbault. "But after I was down there a while, I was made and forced to do these dirty things. So the habit stayed right with me after I ran away…If I was not forced to do these dirty things at the feeble minded school, I would never be behind these prison bars for the rest of my life."

A month after being incarcerated for the Pioletti murder, Brandt received a visit from his mother, brother and a young nephew at the detention ward, where he had been confined. A letter from the deputy warden to the warden regarding the visit noted that "[t]his inmate did not speak over four words to his mother or brother, and when his seven year old nephew stepped in front of him, this inmate's eyes almost came out of his head with a craving to get his hands on this child." The letter added that Brandt started to cry and said, "Please take him away."

Brandt said that the attendants who administered such beatings and sexual abuse upon the boys at Fairbault all quit their jobs just after he ran away for the last time. But as soon as they found out that he'd been put into prison for life, they all got their jobs back, which is why Brandt decided to expose what had been going on there. "I sincerely hope and trust, that knowing what you know now, about these three attendants, you will not stand by and see them ruin the lives of other boys that are down there yet."

After running away from Fairbault the first time, he was readmitted in August 1916 and promptly ran away again. He was sent to the State Training School in Red Wing in October of that year because of "little scrapes." At the end of 1917, Brandt was said to be feigning epileptic fits at Red Wing, which sent him right back to Fairbault.

In a letter to Warden J.J. Sullivan at the prison in Stillwater, Fairbault superintendent G.C. Hanna said that "knowing that this was an open institution from which he could walk away without any hindrance, he evidently put on the seizures at the Training School in order to be transferred."

It does seem odd that Brandt would want to go back to a place he'd already run away from twice; perhaps Red Wing was even worse. The State Training School at Red Wing was pegged as "hell on earth" by an inmate who went on to become one of the country's most brutal and incorrigible serial killers, arsonists and rapists. Carl Panzram, who killed twenty-one men and boys and committed hundreds more rapes of men and boys, arsons and robberies, spent two years at the Minnesota Training School, from 1903 to 1905. He later wrote of his time there as if it was a torture chamber, which included him suffering sexual abuse by a staff member his very first night at the facility. It portended things to come.

Any infraction or failure to learn the lessons or Christian teachings resulted in beatings with wooden planks, leather straps, whips and paddles, he said in a book titled *Malice, Madness, and Mayhem: An Eclectic Collection of American Infamy* by Beverly Roath. After two years there, he convinced the parole board that he'd been reformed, having learned to say what he knew the board wanted to hear. But he later said that "I had learned more about stealing, lying, hating, burning and killing" there.

When Panzram was released at the age of fourteen, "I fully decided when I left there just how I would live my life. I made up my mind that I would rob, burn, destroy and kill everywhere I could and everybody I could as long as I lived." He did just that, running rampant over four continents until he was finally hanged in prison at Leavenworth, Kansas, in 1930.

It is possible that Panzram's treatment at the Minnesota Training School wasn't indicative of the treatment in general there. He may have been an especially bad seed and may have received punishments more severely than other boys there. However, the school did announce publicly in 1912 that "the keen edge of a leather strap" would no longer be used as punishment for gross insubordination at the school, according to a story in the *Oelwein (IA) Daily Register*. "Corporal punishment has given way to moral suasion" as a new superintendent was taking over the facility. So, while the Minnesota Training School for Boys may not have been quite the "torture chamber" of Panzram's experience, it still may not have been all that great a place when Brandt was there twelve years later.

After returning to Fairbault, Brandt promptly ran away for a third time before being returned in July 1918. He escaped a few weeks later and never returned. It wasn't long, though, before he stole a watch from one of his sisters and landed in the Minnesota State Reformatory for Men at St. Cloud. The reformatory had been conceived as an institution for correcting criminal tendencies before they became chronic. It was felt that a younger prisoner could not be reformed by locking him up with the hardened criminals at the state prison at Stillwater, according to the Minnesota Department of Corrections. It didn't work with Brandt.

Another factor working to Brandt's detriment was that he suffered from epileptic psychosis. Epilepsy is a neurological condition that affects the nervous system and causes seizures that are not caused by some known medical condition like alcohol withdrawal or extremely low blood sugar, according to the website epilepsy.com. The seizures in epilepsy may be related to a brain injury or a family tendency, but most of the time the cause is unknown.

A seizure is a sudden surge of electrical activity in the brain that usually affects how a person feels or acts for a short time. Seizures are not a disease in themselves. Instead, they are a symptom of many different disorders that can affect the brain. Some seizures can hardly be noticed, while others are totally disabling. Seizures can vary with the patient. Symptoms can go from blacking out to convulsing violently to difficulty talking, eyes rolling up, heart racing, foot stomping, thoughts racing and many more.

It's most common for people to get epilepsy in their first year of life, so it's probable that Brandt suffered from this his whole life. The website estimates that up to 2 percent of the world's population develops the symptoms.

Factors that can provoke the type of seizures that Brandt had include being exposed to heavy alcohol use, severe psychological stress, deficiencies of vitamins or minerals and a lack of sleep. In the early 1900s, some states had laws forbidding people with epilepsy to marry or become parents, and some states permitted sterilization. Treatment for the disease has gotten much better since Brandt's time. With medication, about half of children outgrow their epilepsy. It is a good bet that Brandt didn't have access to these medications while at home. According to his prison records, it appeared as though Brandt fared better while incarcerated due to medicine and the lack of alcohol.

But Brandt was afflicted by more than just epilepsy, which does not necessarily make people violent or mentally ill. What made Brandt violent were his psychoses. The seizures he suffered from most likely just caused him to black out. Either that or he used them as an excuse "not to remember" what he'd done.

Psychosis, or psychotic disorder, is a severe mental disorder in which the person loses contact with reality. The percentage of those afflicted with epilepsy who also suffer from psychosis is small, notes epilepsy.com. In general, psychotic episodes in people with epilepsy tend to be less severe and respond better to therapy. Symptoms can include seeing, hearing, smelling or tasting things that are not there; paranoia; and delusional thoughts. Depending on the condition underlying the psychotic symptoms, symptoms may be constant or they may come and go. Psychosis can occur as a result of brain injury or disease.

Despite all of his problems, Brandt was generally well oriented, had a good memory and gave the impression of having even better intelligence than his test results indicated, according to a March 1929 letter from F. Kuhlman, director of the research bureau for the Minnesota Department of Public Institutions. Kuhlman had just administered a fourth IQ test to Brandt on which he scored a lifetime low of 49 "because of an evident desire on his part to make a low score." Brandt figured that if he was seen as being mentally deficient, he would not be held as responsible for his crimes, Kuhlman said. This desire of Brandt's to be seen as less responsible for his crimes was noted more than a few times in his prison records.

George H. Freeman, a psychiatrist in the Minnesota prison system who examined Brandt several times, said in January 1927 that Brandt was "well oriented for time, place and person. His memory appears good. Emotionally he possibly appears somewhat depressed. He does not want to talk about his crime and conviction. Says they think he wants to brag about it when he is really sorry and ashamed."

At that time, Freeman said that Brandt was nervous and kept picking at his hands. He said over and over in his evaluations during the time Brandt spent in prison that Brandt was a sexual pervert and an epileptic but wasn't sure that he was psychotic. "He is quite definitely a defective delinquent," Freeman wrote in 1929.

Brandt's shame in committing the Pioletti murder could have caused him to write a letter on March 16, 1926, to the lad's uncle, Reverend Louis Pioletti, pastor at Holy Redeemer Catholic Church in St. Paul. The content of the letter is unknown, and there was no record of a return letter from the pastor.

Brandt was officially received into the Minnesota state prison system on November 17, 1925, having been found guilty of second-degree murder and sentenced to life in prison at the age of twenty-three and assigned prisoner no. 8312.

His health started to deteriorate, and on June 24, 1931, he was transferred to the Asylum for the Dangerous Insane in St. Peter, Minnesota. He died there on August 1 and is buried in the hospital cemetery. The cause of death was listed as "pulmonary tuberculosis" on his death certificate, with a contributing cause listed as epileptic psychosis, both of which the document notes he'd had for several years. His mother and father were not listed on the death certificate. Instead, "Not stated" was listed in the space for the father's name; "Unknown" was in the space for the mother. Brandt's occupation was listed as a laborer.

When he confessed to the Schumacher killing, but it was not believed, authorities noted that if Brandt's confession was indeed substantiated, he would not face any further punishment, as he was already in prison for life. But it "would clear up the case and remove all suspicion from several other men who have been held for investigation," according to a November 26 *Milwaukee Sentinel* story.

Just three days later, Brandt's confession was once again accepted as truth. Detective Kraemer went back to Stillwater on November 28, two days after Thanksgiving, and took along stenographer Charles Engel of the district attorney's staff to question Brandt one more time, according to a November 29 *Milwaukee Sentinel* report. This examination of Brandt lasted four and a half hours, after which Kramer determined that the discrepancies in Brandt's earlier confession were deliberate misstatements.

According to the detective, Brandt told him that he'd intentionally lied about some details of the murder because he thought Wisconsin had capital punishment. Brandt said he didn't want to go back to Milwaukee and be hanged. Although he previously said he'd thrown away Buddy's overalls after the killing, Brandt now said that he had not actually done so. He also now said that he had not hidden the clothing in a culvert, as he at first said. During this questioning, Brandt also revealed details that had not been published in newspapers, according to Engel.

"There is absolutely no doubt but that Brandt is Buddy's slayer," Engel was quoted as saying in the *Journal*. "Brandt's interview Saturday cleared up any doubt which may have existed in our minds as to his guilt. Although he was nervous and excited, and his physical condition is such that he at times became incoherent, there is not the slightest possibility of his having faked the confession. He told us of details which we knew to be true but had for the moment forgotten. He could not have picked those out of thin air." Kraemer echoed Engel's sentiments the following day when he returned to Milwaukee from Stillwater, saying that he was convinced that Brandt had indeed committed the crime.

Because William Brandt was already serving a life term, Wisconsin authorities said that they figured there was no point in charging him with the Schumacher crime. Even if convicted, he'd still spend the rest of his days behind bars. "It would be useless to bring him to trial in Wisconsin," Engel said.

However, there are those who doubted that the police were on the up and up. In a letter that Brandt's brother, Hubert, sent him that was dated November 27, the day that Detective Kraemer said Brandt admitted the whole thing once and for all, Hubert reminded his brother that he believed he didn't kill Buddy Schumacher.

The letter, part of Brandt's prison file, noted: "Now Bill, those illusions & spells you have about that Milwaukee boy you must forget or you will believe you did do it as long as you talk about it & I know you didn't do it."

A little over a year after confessing to Buddy's murder, Brandt once again denied that he had done it. During an examination by Dr. George H. Freeman, the superintendent of St. Peter State Hospital in St. Peter, Minnesota, Brandt said that "the officer" wanted him to admit to the killing. So he did.

Freeman's report reads in part: "He states he worked a couple days in twine shop, was setting down, when the officer wanted him to admit killing a boy in Milwaukee and he owned up to it, provided they didn't tell his people. Says he did not do the crime but as long as he had a life sentence he owned up to it to keep someone else out of trouble." At this time, Brandt also said that he didn't remember killing the Pioletti boy.

The report goes on to say that Brandt launched into "a detached recital of events leading up to the (Pioletti) murder but claims to know nothing of that. Not knowing of the murder, he went home, slept soundly and was arrested the following day. Feels if he had a square deal more of an investigation would have been made. His confession was forced."

Brandt's recanting of his confession may have never made it any further than the warden's office. Not one newspaper article on it could be found. A forced confession would certainly fit in with a lot of what we know. Buddy's pals did not identify Brandt as the man they saw near the railroad tracks on the day Buddy disappeared. When Brandt originally confessed, he had so many of the details incorrect that authorities said that they doubted he was being honest. It took four and a half hours of questioning to get Brandt's second confession, and he later recanted it.

Did police find a patsy to pin this killing on just so they could say they solved it? Or did William Brandt just say that his confession was forced to try to remove some guilt from his shoulders? Did William Brandt kill Buddy Schumacher or not?

Just as authorities felt like they had things wrapped up, another bizarre twist in this tale came up as another man confessed to murdering Buddy Schumacher. Frank Stencel, who was awaiting sentencing in Bryan, Ohio, for breaking into a New York Central railroad station in nearby Stryker, said that he strangled Buddy. In a written confession, Stencel said that "remorse coupled with fear of apprehension through his fingerprints had driven him to confess," according to a United Press story in the December 3 *Stevens Point Daily Journal*.

Milwaukee County undersheriff Kroening sent Deputy Edward Siepman to talk to Stencel. Stencel described the Schumacher murder in fairly good detail, his appearance somewhat matched that described by Buddy's companions and he had quite a lengthy criminal history using various names. Anthony Stencel, one of the names he'd used, was arrested in Detroit in 1910 for breaking into a home. He had served a term in prison in Jackson, Michigan, in 1911 and 1912. In 1916, he was arrested on a burglary charge in Cleveland and was sent to the Ohio State Reformatory. He was in Wisconsin around the time Buddy had been killed. He'd also been in Minneapolis about the time another youngster was killed in some woods there.

But after talking with the Milwaukee police, Stencel changed his mind on the matter, claiming that he'd read of the murder in newspapers. Like Brandt, Stencel was also seen by authorities as a man of lesser mental capacity, and a fellow prison mate of Stencel's told a reporter, "That bird is certainly cuckoo."

Police said that they seriously doubted Stencel's confession, and a December 4 *Milwaukee Sentinel* story noted that the confession was false and that the man only knew of the murder from reading newspapers, according to a telegram sent from Bryan, Ohio, by Siepman.

Just like Brandt, Stencel changed his testimony after talking to Milwaukee police. Since authorities had already told the public that they'd accepted Brandt's confession, did they now convince Stencel to rescind his confession?

Was Frank Stencel the real killer of Buddy Schumacher?

Chapter 17

MORE VIOLENCE AGAINST KIDS

For a time after the Schumacher killing, other disappearances or murders of children in the Milwaukee area either reminded people of Buddy or led them to believe that Buddy's killer might still be at large. Two such instances happened less than a month after Brandt confessed.

Eight-year-old Mike Lecher, who lived on Milwaukee's west side, went out the evening of Sunday, December 13, with his older sister and younger brother, as well as some friends, as they'd been told that Santa Claus was giving out candy on a busy corner in the city. The children found no Santa Claus and started home. Mike's brother and sister headed off from the group and then the other boys left. Mike, alone, headed for his house but didn't make it there.

A few days later, his mother was sure that he was dead. "We'll never see him again," Mary Leeher said. "In my heart of hearts I can feel that my boy is gone forever."

The story then referenced the Schumacher murder: "A moron murder, a fate like that of little Arthur Schumacher, who was killed last summer near his home in Wauwatosa, was feared by the police."

This story received similar coverage to the Schumacher case in the Milwaukee papers. The December 16 *Milwaukee Sentinel* published a front-page story on the Lecher disappearance with a large headline, "8-Year-Old Boy Disappears in Search for Santa Claus." Included was a photo of the grieving family—Mike's parents and brother and sister huddled together at their home, with a photo of Mike inset, eerily reminiscent of the photo of the Schumacher family earlier in the year.

The very next day, the *Milwaukee Sentinel*'s top story was about another eight-year-old west-side Milwaukee boy named Roy Tolzmann who was reported missing, as well as an eleven-year-old south-side girl who "narrowly escaped death by strangulation when her assailant sought to force a handkerchief down her throat," bringing yet another vivid reminder of Buddy. "ANOTHER BOY MISSING!" the headline across the front page screamed in disbelief.

Once again, police were dispatched into the cold Milwaukee night to search for a pair of "degenerates," this time looking for those who could lead them to either Lecher or Tolzmann. In a reprise of the first night of the Schumacher search, the night of Wednesday, December 16, had two groups of people out searching Milwaukee neighborhoods for the missing boys.

While Lecher's parents watched out the windows of their home at 3008 Canal Street down the bluffs that line the Menomonee River Valley and the Milwaukee Road, police with flashlights scoured the area. Meanwhile, detectives and police officers searched barns and old buildings and questioned scores of people for clues to Roy Tolzmann's disappearance near Seventeenth and Walnut Streets, where residents still had vivid recollections of an attack on a young girl there a couple of years ago.

The Tolzmann boy was last seen with an old friend of the family, Jack Steinert, who had given him and his sister, Gladys, both a dime when he saw them after school about a block from their home. Gladys ran home with her dime; Steinert said that he last saw Roy running across the street to the candy store. Roy never got to the store, though.

The *Sentinel* story raised nearly the same questions about Roy Tolzmann's disappearance as had been raised regarding Buddy's: "What happened? Was Roy run down by an automobilist who picked him up, probably mortally injured, and disposed of the body? Was he lured away by a degenerate? Or did he go somewhere to play and meet with an accident?" Meanwhile, authorities were afraid that the Lecher lad, said to be a "frail youngster" by his mother, might have fallen in deep snow on the bluffs of the valley and froze to death.

The story discussed how those investigating Lecher's and Tolzmann's disappearances found "a certain similarity in the two mysteries which rival the disappearance and the subsequent murder of 8-year-old Arthur Schumacher in Wauwatosa last summer."

In the Lecher case, police had some clues to go on: a spot of blood at the foot of the cellar stairway in the building where the Lecher family lived and a conversation between two "negroes" at a Milwaukee police station in which one reportedly told the other about Mikey's disappearance an hour before the parents began to search for the child.

Unlike the Schumacher case, which dragged on for nearly two months before the body was found, the Mike Lecher and Roy Tolzmann cases were wrapped up within a matter of a few days, neither very pleasantly.

Lecher was found the morning of December 17 locked in an abandoned railroad car, hungry and suffering from exposure from two or three nights in the frigid Milwaukee winter. On one of the nights, the temperature had dropped as low as thirteen degrees and was never above freezing for the past few days. Nearly unclothed, he lay huddled on a pile of straw in the car, a Winnebago that had been a diner and buffet car before being retired seven years earlier. The car sat on the tracks in the "boneyard," was boarded up and had no windows. Doctors determined that he'd been "criminally," or sexually, assaulted. The boy was found just about three blocks from his home.

Later that day, Roy Tolzmann was found. He wasn't as fortunate as Lecher. Tolzmann's bones were found in a burned barn on Paul or Fred Hartung's property off Lisbon Road and Sixty-third Street in the town of Wauwatosa. The barn had burned the night he had disappeared. Roy's head, arms and legs had been hacked from the body with a hay knife before it was left in the barn to burn. In the *Milwaukee Sentinel*, pathologist Edward Milosavich said that this was the work of a "human fiend." Roy's blackened belt buckle, which was found at the scene, was identified by his mother, helping to determine that this was indeed the boy in question.

Police solved the Tolzmann murder quickly, as Jack Steinert—a twenty-six-year-old convicted felon with a long history of problems with the law and considered mentally ill—confessed to the killing the day after the body was found. He had served five years in the Green Bay Reformatory for sexually assaulting a newsboy at gunpoint in 1919 and told investigators that he had lured Roy Tolzmann away with the promise of giving him presents.

Steinert admitted that he had indeed given Roy and Gladys dimes and sent them on their way. He made a deal with Roy to meet up with him later on, when he would get Roy a toy train that the boy had coveted for Christmas. By the time they met up again, Steinert had gotten drunk on several "moonshines" at a local "blind pig." He and the boy took a streetcar to the northwest side of the city and on into the town of Wauwatosa. Steinert admitted choking the boy to death after Roy started screaming and lit fire to the barn, although he said that he couldn't say if he had hacked the boy's appendages from his body. "I wasn't in my right mind. I don't know. I wouldn't say that I did it and I wouldn't say that I didn't do it."

Justice moved swiftly. It took just thirty hours after Steinert's confession to sentence him to life plus twenty years at the prison at Waupun for murder, arson and sexual abuse of the boy.

During the investigation of the Tolzmann murder, police questioned Steinert about two other Milwaukee child murders—Godfrey Dionizi and Buddy Schumacher. Steinert, who had been in court sixteen times before he was convicted in 1919, didn't serve the entire sentence for the newsboy attack and was out of prison by December 22, 1919, about three months before Dionizi's body was found the following March near the same culvert where Steinert had attacked the newsboy. Steinert said that he was in Minneapolis looking for a job when Dionizi was killed, adding that he had nothing to hide since he was going to prison for life anyway.

Police asked Steinert about his whereabouts when Buddy Schumacher disappeared, too, even though they had said they were already convinced that they had Buddy's killer locked away in Minnesota for life. Emil Tolzmann, Roy's father, told police that he and Steinert were working a construction job near the scene of the Schumacher murder on the day the boy disappeared. Time sheets showed that Steinert worked up until 4:00 p.m. that day, but nobody could say if he might have been able to slip away during the day long enough to commit the crime.

"I'd tell you if I did," Steinert said. "There wouldn't be any use holding out now. I'm a cooked goose and I'll be on the inside looking out from now on. Another murder or two wouldn't make any difference; it's life anyway you look at it. But I didn't do it."

At the conclusion of the grilling, Milwaukee police captain Harry McCrory said that he was satisfied that Steinert didn't have anything to do with the Dionizi and Schumacher killings.

It took about two more weeks for police to capture little Mikey Lecher's attacker. The boy was able to give police a description of the man, a black man perhaps in his sixties with three fingers on one hand whom Lecher had heard others call "Three-Fingered Dad." Rufus E. Brown, sixty-three, who had had problems getting a job as a porter on the railroad, hopped on a freight train a few hours after Mike went missing. A fairly large man in poor physical health, Brown was apprehended in Davenport, Iowa, and sent back to Milwaukee, where he was identified by the boy from his hospital bed.

At first, Brown denied it. But the following day, on New Year's Eve 1925, Brown confessed. "I'm guilty and I'm ready to pay the penalty," the *Sentinel* quoted Brown as saying "in his negro dialect." "The truth comes hard but I did it," Brown continued. "I took the boy down into the railroad yards and into the old car and left him there. I thought that he would die and that his body wouldn't be found until I could get far from Milwaukee." It was expected that Brown would serve out the rest of his days in prison, as the kidnapping charge could get him fifteen years, while the assault charges could have gotten him one to twenty-five years. At his age and health, he was not expected to ever get out of jail.

It should not come as a surprise that like Steinert, Brandt, Stencel and Vreeland, Brown was also considered mentally ill. He had spent time in an insane asylum in Dunning, Illinois, for "degenerate tendencies" and told police that he had been labeled "incurable" there. Brown was hazy on the details but said that he was released on parole. He had spent some time in Madison, Wisconsin, and was sought for months by authorities there for attacks on two young boys, having fled the city after both occurrences.

Not only were these five men all mentally ill, they all knew they were, too. They knew that sexually abusing boys was wrong, though none seemed to be capable of stopping himself. At least, they said they couldn't.

In a lengthy story in the December 18, 1925 *Milwaukee Sentinel*, reporter George Archer detailed Steinert's account of his past in which Steinert blamed a reform school for some of his criminal tendencies, complaining that society inflames such passions as he has and saying that death is the only way to stop him and his kind. In a prolonged interview in front of newspaper men and police, Steinert also indicated that moonshine liquor was an inflamer of the pervert in him and that when it killed his mind, he knew not what he was doing.

The reporter said that Steinert "spoke on the whole without hesitation, pausing only when his weak mentality could not frame the words to express the thoughts that were rushing in his head."

Steinert said that his life started to spiral downward after he left school after seventh grade at the age of thirteen and joined a gang in 1915. They stole cars and took them for joy rides and got caught, he said. "I think I was as good as the average boy when I left school and my first temptation came from the suggestion of a gang," Steinert added. He was sentenced to the Boys Industrial School in Waukesha, where Steinert said he "was coached by my fellow inmates in the practices that have brought me here today." Two years after getting out of the reform school, Steinert was back in jail for the attack on the newsboy. In one report, Steinert was asked if he'd been sentenced to Green Bay for "tampering with 14 boys." He said he wasn't quite sure of the number. It was also revealed that at some point, Steinert had also been sentenced to a workhouse for forgery.

Steinert went on to discuss the reasons he decided to attack Roy Tolzmann that day. He said that he had read of the disappearance of Mike Lecher, perhaps at the hands of one of his kind, in the newspapers. "You know that inflames our minds," he said of reading the article, "and then and there I determined that I would go that very day and do the same thing."

It was noted by Archer in this story, however, that news of the Lecher disappearance was not made public until after Roy Tolzmann's murder, and therefore Steinert couldn't have known about it through news coverage.

When asked if he was sorry for what he'd done, Steinert asked if he'd be believed. He then stuttered, "I, I, I…I was not in my right mind when I choked that boy. Believe it or not, people like me don't know what we do in the heat of passion."

Archer reported that detectives in the audience smiled grimly at the phrase "heat of passion" as they feared that Steinert would try to say he'd not been sane at the time of the killing and use that excuse to get the charge lessened to second-degree murder, which would only carry a twenty-five-year sentence.

Before leaving the interview, Steinert made a suggestion as to what should be done with people who committed the types of crimes he did. "I believe that all of my kind should be put away for life or even killed to get us out of the way. They ought to sterilize us."

A clipping of an editorial in an unknown newspaper found in William Brandt's prison records suggested the same thing. It read in part that the reason he was allowed to plead guilty to second-degree murder instead of first-degree in the Pioletti case was "so that maudlin sentimentalists and the 'sob sisters' could urge an early pardon because the brute 'was and is sick and must be humanely treated.'"

The editorial concluded by noting, "We trust that this case will stimulate the agitation for the restoration of the death penalty. A few more occurrences like the Brandt case will surely bring it about."

After Steinert's interview, as he was being led back to his cell, his mother, Minnie Krenske, met him. "How could you do it, John?" she asked her son. At that, she started sobbing, and Steinert wept the first tears he had shed since he murdered the Tolzmann boy, according to Archer's story.

"This is a swell Christmas you're giving us," Steinert's stepfather, Ernst Krenske, said to him before pressing three packs of cigarettes into Steinert's hand. His mother's gift was her handkerchief, with which he wiped the tears from his eyes as he walked away.

Steinert confessed to all three counts against him to municipal court judge George A. Shaughnessy. In passing sentence on Steinert, Shaughnessy reiterated what many felt of Jack Steinert and the other types who had committed sexually violent crimes against the area's youth recently:

> *As early as a year ago, I advocated segregation of men of your type. I am informed that your case is not a question of insanity; insanity in this case means that a person must have hallucination or illusions. You have neither. You will go through life infected with degenerate impulses and should you beget children, they too will be degenerate. You must realize that men of your type are a menace to the community, that while you and your kind are at large youth is not safe. It is the duty of this court or any other court to remove from society for all time, those of your ilk.*
>
> *It is a duty that I owe to society and I'm going to see that you are never free again. In this state a life sentence means about 30 years. I don't know what the future authorities may do in your case as regards parole but I shall say to them that you must never be released.*

When Shaughnessy imposed the sentence, not only did he give Steinert the life-plus-twenty-year term, he also decreed that the killer must spend every December 15 throughout the term in solitary confinement to coincide with the date of the killing. As Steinert left the courtroom, puffing on a cigarette, he was ushered out a side door into an office in city hall. There, among court officials, sat Roy Tolzmann's parents. As he passed, Mrs. Tolzmann "suddenly grew tense, rose with a demoniacal yell and threw herself at Steinert. It took her husband, Emil, and three court attachés to hold her, for her strength was almost superhuman," according to the *Journal* story. "Her yells continued for 10 minutes and re-echoed throughout the corridors of the city hall."

One has to wonder if Florence Schumacher had met up with Buddy's killer in such a manner if she would have reacted similarly. It was apparent that some members of the public had feelings like Mrs. Tolzmann had when Steinert was loaded into a sheriff's automobile under a guard of deputies and driven off toward the state prison in Waupun on December 19. A crowd of about 150 people had gathered outside the county jail, and the vociferous throng repeatedly yelled, "Kill him" and "Lynch him" as deputies cleared a path for the car to pass and prevented any unruly outbreak.

Clearly, though, the public's anger toward such men was very high.

Chapter 18

THE "MORON" DANGER

Due to the instances of violence against Milwaukee-area children by "degenerates or morons" in the second half of 1925, a spotlight was thrust on the issue of the mental illness there.

Some mentally ill were wandering the country. It was not uncommon for men, whose mental illness caused them to lose their jobs and their families, to hitchhike or use the nation's railroads and highways to go from place to place seeking odd jobs or fellow "hobos" with whom to commiserate and beg, borrow or steal.

The "Golden Age of the Hobo" is generally defined as the time between the 1880s and World War I. But many men were still riding the rails in the mid-1920s, and with improved roads, they had started picking up rides in automobiles, too.

Meanwhile, the era in which Buddy Schumacher lived was also the beginning of an era in which mental diseases were starting to be viewed differently. It was not until the 1920s and '30s that mental hospitals in the United States, even expensive private ones, offered differential diagnosis and treatment based, at least in part, on scientific understandings. Until this time, most such institutions were called insane asylums.

During the 1920s, Sigmund Freud's psychoanalytic ideas became increasingly influential in the United States. Psychoanalysis emphasized the importance of early childhood experiences and their impact on mental health later in life. Combine these developments with the fact that the Milwaukee County institutions were so close to the Schumacher home, and there was much talk of the mental well-being of vagrants one might meet nearby.

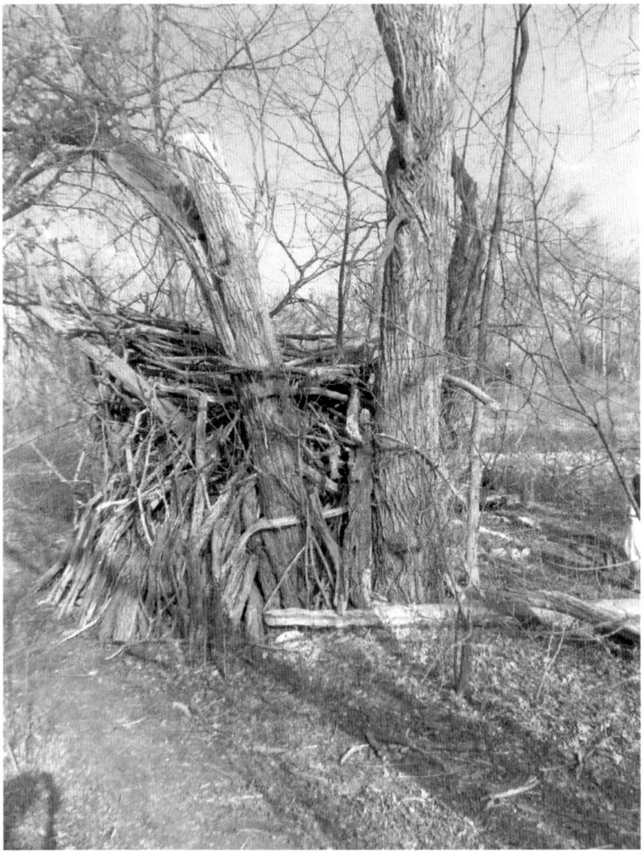

Children have built some shelters along the banks of the Menomonee River near the old swimming hole. In the 1920s, homeless men used to set up similar shelters in the area, which used to be much more overgrown with bushes and tall reeds.

Stories and editorials dotted the local newspapers at the end of 1925 and the beginning of 1926, pleading for some sort of changes to the mental healthcare system, blaming a wanton society and warning parents to keep closer watch on their children.

Shortly after William Brandt confessed to killing Buddy, the *Sheboygan Press* published an editorial titled "The Moron Danger," which must have summed up fairly well the feelings of many Wisconsin residents at the time:

> *In the case of this William Brandt, an investigation of his habits show that he has been mentally unbalanced for a number of years—another one of those monstrosities that are allowed to roam the highways without interference. All too frequently parents with an abnormal youth in the family are reluctant to have him confined in a state institution, even though it be best for him and all concerned.*

> *A lad who is deficient in those things that go to make up the normal youth should be confined and given treatment. You cannot tell when one of these defectives will do the unexplainable thing. No parent has the right to jeopardize the welfare of the community and endanger the lives of little tots by keeping one of these misfits at home. We have too many experiences of late, all of which have resulted in some of the most fiendish crimes in the annals of American criminology. Our laws should be so strengthened that a complete check can be kept on the mental condition of each individual. Parents who are loath to confine a son who is mentally defective, are doing themselves an injury as well as the community. State institutions are maintained with the idea of according treatment.*
>
> *We do not know whether the confession of William Brandt is to be relied upon or not, but that Arthur Schumacher was murdered by a degenerate is beyond question, and the fact that Brandt is serving time for a similar crime indicates that he is one of the worst moron types.*
>
> *On October 13th last, the body of Francis Pioletti, 11, Italian boy, was discovered mutilated in the attic of a St. Paul home. Brandt was identified as the person who had taken the Italian youth into the deserted house.*
>
> *In today's Press we have a cartoon that we want each reader to study with a view of awakening him to a better understanding of the seriousness of this new condition of affairs. We are the guardians of the boys and girls who are sent on their way to school each day, and as such we ought to put safeguards around them to the end that they can travel the highways with a fair degree of safety. Usually one of these defectives resides in the community, and we have no right to harbor or allow him to be harbored in our midst. He is better off in an institution where medical treatment can be accorded, for at home he is a burden upon the other members of the family and a constant danger to them.*

In a story in the *Milwaukee Journal* on December 10, 1925, District Attorney Wengert suggested that national record crime rates would not come down simply by increasing punishments. A report by the U.S. attorney general's office two days earlier noted that crime in America had risen more than 33 percent since the start of the decade.

"As long as there is not a change of heart in the rank and file of people there will be little change for the better. Punishment in itself doesn't change criminals. Our educational system creates desires, but does not create the ability to satisfy those desires. Our system does not instill in the minds of our young people the sympathy and respect that would protect them from criminal careers," Wengert said. "Any change of conditions, except those which bring a change of heart will be a feeble effort."

After several months' urging by social agencies for the establishment of a mental clinic, the Milwaukee County Board judiciary committee on December 14 approved several new positions to make up the staff of a new mental hygiene facility. This was called "a blow to perverts like Jack Steinert" by the *Milwaukee Sentinel*.

Wengert issued a warning to parents that appeared in an article in the *Milwaukee Sentinel* on December 18, the same edition in which the Tolzmann murder was reported. He said that while his office and the police and sheriff's forces would continue to do all in their power to safeguard the city's children and punish those guilty of attacks, he also asked that parents use every reasonable precaution in the supervision of their children, while at the same time he tried to calm fears.

"It is a revolting situation indeed when two young boys (Tolzmann and Lecher) are made the victims of fiendish attacks within a period of twenty-four hours," Wengert said. "Men of the type responsible for crimes of this kind are at large the country over. They are not always unemployed and sometimes are respected members of a community who have been able to conceal their treachery. There is nothing about them which can expose them until they are actually connected with an attack."

Wengert said that there was no cause for extreme alarm before adding that "parents should at all times know where their children are and what they are doing as a matter of proper supervision. Boys and girls should be taught that under no consideration should they associate with strangers. The parents should know everyone the children know. Children should not play in out-of-the-way places, where men are working or where vagrants might pass by or congregate."

The *Milwaukee Sentinel* alleged in a December 19 editorial that authorities knew well ahead of the Schumacher and Tolzmann killings that the men responsible had no business being out in public, and had there been a mental institution for these kinds of men, the boys would still be alive. The editorial also suggested that the cost of building an institution of this sort, and running it, would be less than the cost to society of letting these men serve shortened sentences and return to society without determining whether they were any better off than when they were committed.

"To parents who suffer as bereaved Milwaukee fathers and mothers have suffered in the last six months, there is no such thing as cost—it is beyond that," the editorial noted. "If this situation were something that could not be corrected, that would be different. But it isn't. A psychopathic laboratory to decide the mental condition of those who come within the law's reaches would be the first step. The second would be a law to permit segregation and retention of the degenerate so long as his degeneracy persisted. Is that too hard a nut for society to crack? A business man, faced by some similar problem, would solve it in 24 hours."

An editorial in the *Milwaukee Sentinel* two days later titled "Help Protect the Child" echoed Wengert's warnings for parents. It also gave instructions for children on how to lessen the chances that they could become targets or victims of the type that had been preying on area youths in recent months, as well as suggestions for community members on how to properly interact with children:

> *It is natural for parents to feel a bit of pride when their children are noticed in public and when the children themselves show ability to meet strangers in a well mannered way. Or when children come in to tell how someone has been nice to them on the street.*
>
> *But the terrible events in Milwaukee in the last few days only serve to emphasize the dangers of casual friendships contracted by children. Nine hundred and ninety-nine of these friendships may be all right, but in the thousandth lies disaster. So parents should make it their duty to know who their children are meeting, and to instruct them about associating with strangers. The method of the moral leper is to start by giving the child candy or an ice cream cone or a dime. Having won the child's confidence, the pervert is able to entice him away. The degenerate doesn't attack the child in the street unless his degeneracy has drifted into insanity; he uses the shrewder method.*
>
> *If every parent in Milwaukee will instruct his children never to go away with a stranger or receive favors from a stranger, or make an acquaintance without telling about it at home, much good may result. The child should courteously but firmly refuse and then should move rapidly away. It is the only safe course.*
>
> *And well meaning people who take pleasure in noticing children and doing them little favors will help a good deal by "reforming" themselves. They should not try to break down the child's reserve, which the parent has built up for the child's protection. If you want to do things for children, do them for the children of your acquaintances, who know and trust you. Don't use a method that plays into the hands of the degenerate.*

This advice wouldn't have saved Roy Tolzmann's life, as his killer had known him for a year, his father for two years and had worked for his grandfather; Jack Steinert was considered a family friend by that point. But it may have helped others.

The same day as that editorial appeared in the *Journal*, the *Sentinel* published a similar editorial, taking off on Wengert's warnings, too. The *Sentinel* editorial also commented on what a jolt these recent crimes had been for Milwaukee: "The revelation of degeneracy being at large and able to stain the Christmas season with the slaughter of innocent children comes with a particular shock to this city, which has always been remarkably free from crime and is fully determined to maintain its good record for a high degree of public safety."

The editorial remarked that while the police would do everything they could do to make the streets safe for children, those efforts needed to be supplemented by parental supervision, which would certainly be forthcoming considering recent events. Much discussion as to what to do with these so-called morons was going to be needed, the paper noted. But while all those proposals were being studied, something needed to be done immediately to protect the children under existing conditions.

"While there is no emergency and no need for alarm," the editorial read, "the existence of potential criminals must be recognized and guarded against by vigilance in homes, aided by schools, impressing children with the necessity of taking no chances and refusing to be misled by suspicious strangers. The lesson of caution is dearly bought, as it is, by two sacrifices."

In that same newspaper, the *Sentinel* wrote of a local Presbyterian pastor who, during a "scathing denunciation of modern depravity" in his sermon to his congregation the day before, said that "had Jack Steinert been willing to know and acknowledge Christ, Roy Tolzmann would be alive today, and Waupun would have one less name on its roll."

Reverend J.H. Miller of Perseverance Presbyterian Church in Milwaukee was one of several clergymen whose sermons that Sunday were attended by *Sentinel* reporters. Of the church services that reporters attended, Miller was most scathing in his comments, perhaps because he performed the funeral service for Roy Tolzmann at his church at Eighteenth and Walnut Streets.

"While we worship God with happy and joyful hearts today," Miller said to his congregation, "let us turn our thoughts to the Tolzmann home… and remember that without a moral consciousness any man is capable of heinous crimes and that the only sure way to prevent repetition of such tragedies is to carry the gospel of Christ into the heart of every man," adding that "Christ has done more to lift the moral and spiritual in man than toward any other realm."

Most of the other preachers preferred to simply discuss the good things that Jesus Christ could do for people and didn't get into any political commentary. In fact, Reverend E.F. Schueler at Cross Evangelical Church at Sixtieth Street and Fond du Lac Avenue went so far as to express that very sentiment. "Christ did not command his church to air and ventilate current events," he told his flock. "Political, social and economic problems must have their place but let the Christian pulpit mind its business." He went on to say, "Blessed and happy may that congregation be which can say of its house of worship, as did the patriarch of old: 'This is none other but the house of God.' That is more than can be said of many a church building in this day and age of ours."

It seemed that everyone, including the "moral leper" himself in some cases, favored segregating such men and locking them up for life unless they could prove that their predatory tendencies had ceased. Several public officials were cited in a December 18, 1925 *Milwaukee Sentinel* story supporting such measures. Milwaukee chief of police Jacob J. Laubenheimer Jr., District Attorney Eugene Wengert, county health commissioner John P. Koehler, Judge Joseph Padway and Wisconsin state senator Oscar Morris all expressed similar sentiments in the story.

Koehler said that degenerates should be treated as having a contagious disease and should be quarantined for life. Morris added that he would introduce legislation pertaining to this if judges would draw it up. Meanwhile, Laubenheimer lamented the fact that some of these sexual crimes carried with them sentences too short. "Under the law the maximum that can be given a man for sodomy is seven years. It should be life," the police chief said. "I do not mean necessarily that these men should be in penal institutions. Perhaps the hospital for the criminal insane is the place. Certainly they should be in some institution to protect boys and girls."

Laubenheimer noted that crimes of this nature seemed to be on the rise in the United States, saying that part of the reason was that the law didn't aptly deal with these types of criminals. "They are permitted to run at large because they are so often believed to be harmless," he said. "They are permitted to multiply. Heredity has something to do with it. One man in two generations may taint a whole strain and produce a dozen with that mental and physical taint which makes them potential criminals."

While most medical experts today say that a desire to sexually abuse children isn't hereditary, abusers do tend to have been physically or sexually abused themselves.

Wengert, meanwhile, called these sexual predators of children functional in society, but incurable, and hoped the institution that was set up would employ these men somehow. "They should be segregated in an institution which could be self supporting," he said. "They are not imbeciles. They are capable of working, but in them is a strain of criminality which can be easily inflamed and which produces the crimes of horror such as we have here before us in Milwaukee today." Wengert also said that this type of mental and physical degeneracy could be detected. He said all criminals should be tested. If they are found to exhibit these strains of degeneracy, they should be put in this institution.

Whatever might cause a man to be prone to such activity, many felt that the environment a man was exposed to could either stem these desires or inflame them. An editorial in the December 18 *Milwaukee Sentinel* spoke directly to this subject, addressing the future in the wake of the Schumacher and Tolzmann murders and the Lecher attack, all three of which involved sexual molestation of children. The editorial lamented the fact that after crimes such as these, the public becomes outraged and police officers go on a manhunt. After the crime is solved and the criminal punished, the American public settles back until the next one.

It went on to discuss what the "fiend" is and what causes him: "The fiend is a product of both heredity and environment. Tainted blood, warped mentality. As the child of these strains grows up it comes in contact with its environment, as we all do. If that environment is wholesome, the defects may be overcome; if unwholesome, degeneracy results. Such processes are going on all the time, in all stations of our life."

The editorial admitted that there was not a whole lot anyone could yet do in preventing these "tainted strains," but "cannot we do something by looking into the environmental influences that contribute to degeneracy?" Those negative influences: "the poison-selling bootlegger is one; the show house (burlesque theater) that panders to passion and nothing but passion, with no thought of art, is another; the poison-laden, so-called 'art' magazine is third; conditions that create drifters are a fourth. All these influences together might not produce degeneracy in a healthy-minded individual. But they lead the defective straight downward."

The editorial noted that all these forces probably couldn't be curbed immediately. "But as we stand, shocked and outraged, can we not at least face the future with the resolution that the things which kill manhood and feed degeneracy shall not go on forever in their destroying work?"

Meanwhile, a report in the *Milwaukee Sentinel* on May 6, 1926, concluded that insanity was on the rise in Milwaukee County and suggested that it may have been tied to prohibition:

> *Insanity in Milwaukee county is on the increase and has been gaining steadily ever since prohibition became effective. The hospital for mental diseases at Wauwatosa is crowded to the doors and sixty patients have been "farmed out" to other asylums in the state.*
>
> *The asylum for chronic insane is likewise crowded.*
>
> *The county infirmary population is far greater than it was in other years; the county hospital is housing more patients than ever before and there is a noticeable increase in the number of children being cared for at the home for dependent children. Incidentally, the Muirdale and Blue Mound tuberculosis sanatoriums are taxed to capacity.*
>
> *These facts were revealed yesterday by William L. Coffey, manager of the Milwaukee county institutions.*

In early 1927, less than two years after the Buddy Schumacher killing, Wisconsin state senator Bernhard "Ben" Gettelman introduced a bill that would provide "a special institution for permanent confinement of morons, degenerates and perverts of the type that commit abnormal and revolting crimes." Gettelman—who as a deputy sheriff in 1919 investigated Jack Steinert's attack on the newsboy and got a confession from the perpetrator—introduced the bill as a campaign promise made "when feeling ran high following the moron murders of two small boys Roy Tolzmann and Arthur (Buddy) Schumacher, who were killed in an uncontrollable frenzy, not intentionally, but to still their outcries," a story in the January 11, 1927 *Milwaukee Sentinel* reported.

At that time, Gettelman said that there had been a clamor for such an institution to be built to help protect the area's youth "against the menace of men known to be as dangerous as Yunkle beasts but for whom the law makes no provision." He and Milwaukee chief of police Laubenheimer urged civic and women's organizations that had appealed for some corrective measure at the time of the Tolzmann and Schumacher cases to add their support to the proposed new law. At this time, such crimes were regarded by the law only as misdemeanors.

Gettelman's proposal would prevent the release of inmates in this institution by governor's pardon or by action of the county board of control. A board of examining physicians would be the supreme power, the only authority for release. Commitment to the facility would be for life or until such time as the physicians approve liberation. Laubenheimer agreed.

"It should be made impossible for 'pull,' money or any other influence to have a bearing on liberating a man once it was found necessary to confine him in this institution," Laubenheimer said.

Building the facility might cost $300,000, but Gettelman said that "the money should not be considered if its expenditure would be the means of saving the life of one child." The senator went on to say that "without a law of this kind the police are powerless. A degenerate is apprehended and found to be the most dangerous type, but the penalty is from ninety days to five years imprisonment, and then he is released—as dangerous as he was before."

Gettelman cited the Tolzmann crime on this specific point. Steinert had been released just two years after being paroled early from a five-year sentence for a similar crime—only the previous crime didn't result in death, the senator noted. Had a hospital of this type been available when Steinert was sentenced for sexually assaulting the newsboy, he might have never gotten out and committed any more such crimes.

"Many men of this type should be regarded more as unfortunates than criminals," Gettelman said. "In Steinert's case he was torn by a Jekyll-Hyde conflict within himself in which his evil complex finally prevailed. A cure might be accomplished in Steinert's case and in the cases of many who are admitted as he is. What some of these men need is rehabilitation by a careful course of treatment. Others are hopeless."

EPILOGUE

Even though two men confessed to killing Buddy Schumacher, the case was said to be unsolved by the Schumacher family, said Keith Egloff. And a newspaper report in 1959 also called it unsolved. After all these years, with all the advances in technology available now, is it possible to determine who killed Arthur "Buddy" Schumacher?

Not likely. But according to one of America's leading DNA experts, "every time I said it can't be done, I've learned to regret it," said Greg Hampikian, professor of biology and criminal justice at Boise State University. Hampikian is also involved in helping exonerate the wrongfully imprisoned as a DNA expert for the Georgia Innocence Project and director of the Idaho Innocence Project.

According to Hampikian, in order to solve this mystery through DNA, there must be some evidence that has been saved somewhere with the killer's DNA on it, in addition to blood relatives of the killer who would be willing to have their DNA compared to the evidence.

"You have to find somebody who saved something," he said.

In this case, it looks like there is no evidence to test. Wauwatosa police have said that they have no records before 1934. These records would have included the handkerchief used to suffocate Buddy, as well as any clothing the boy was wearing when he was found. One would think that any DNA from body fluids the murderer may have left on the boy would have degraded in the eighty-five years since the body was placed in the Wauwatosa Cemetery.

Perhaps, Hampikian suggested, evidence from the case could be in a spot that police are not aware of, misplaced through the years. He said he's run into situations such as this. Or there may be something at the site the body was found—a button perhaps—that was left by the killer. A sweep by a metal detector or a dig with an archaeologist might unearth a clue. While it is not likely to yield DNA, identifying evidence of any sort would be helpful.

Considering the rough maps and descriptions of the place in the woods where the body was found, this undertaking seems fairly large scale and probably would not be worth the time and money to undertake. Additionally, a road has been built through the area, as well as athletic facilities. The spot where the body was found may be covered with asphalt, blacktop or bleachers now.

Finding relatives of the main suspects in the case—William Brandt and Edward Vreeland—has proven extremely difficult. Two of Brandt's relatives declined to speak to me. Convincing them to submit DNA samples may be next to impossible. Even if this were achieved, we would still need to match this DNA to the killer's. After so much time has passed, and considering the way the evidence was handled back then, this is an extremely unlikely scenario.

Even though it may not be possible to solve the mystery for sure, we do know that some good things came from this tragedy. "Mother [Jeanette Schumacher Egloff] said that the one good thing that happened as a result of the murder was that the city cleaned up the area and eventually made a park there," Keith Egloff said.

In early April 1926, about five months after Buddy's body was found, Wauwatosa police chief George Baltes banned vagrants from his city. A two-paragraph story in the *Wauwatosa News* detailed the declaration:

> *The city of Wauwatosa will be kept clean of wanderers of the road, or otherwise known as box car tourists. George Baltes, chief of police, has issued orders to all policemen that an eagle eye should be kept open for this kind of tourist, and to give them orders to move along as soon they set foot inside the city.*
>
> *A special watch will be kept on those places that have been used as hang-outs in the past years. Chief Baltes still has the "Buddy" Schumacher case on his mind and requests that those children who are in the habit of playing along the Menomonee river to notify police of any suspicious looking characters loitering around. In this way, he states, the police and sheriff force will be these nomads.*

It wasn't long after this that the city started clearing away its "yunkles" along the Menomonee River and upgrading its parks, giving its children more safe places to play.

By the end of 1933, a $50,000 concrete public swimming pool had been approved for Hoyt Park near the site of Blackridge, the mud-bottom swimming hole that Buddy and his pals sought the day he disappeared. The pool, one of the Wisconsin public works projects approved by the state

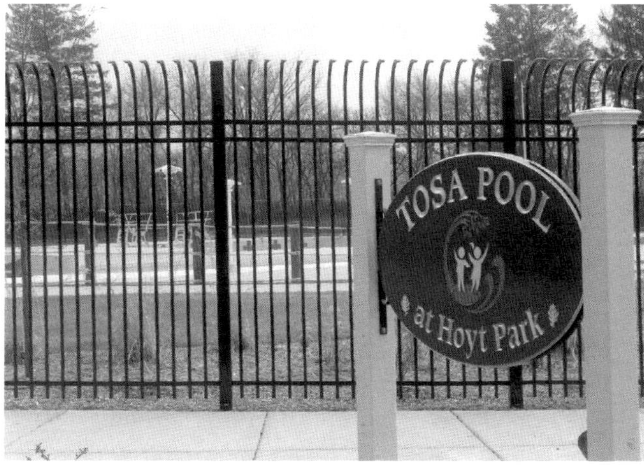

The Tosa Pool at Hoyt Park stands near the site of the old swimming hole. A pool opened at the site in 1939 before closing due to structural problems. A new pool was built a few years later.

advisory board on public works on December 1 of that year, was built on an island in the river, with a bridge connecting the mainland with the island. The pool was officially opened on July 1, 1939. Later, part of the island was filled in so that the river now curves around the pool area.

What happened to Buddy's friends who were with him on the train when he disappeared? John "Jake" Wolf, the oldest of the boys said to have gone on that freight train with Buddy, spent his life working for the railroad, although he never learned to read or write, according to his grandson, Anthony May of Port Washington, Wisconsin. John lived on the northwest side of Milwaukee. He and his wife, Mary, never had children of their own but did raise foster children, and they adopted Anthony's mother. "He was a great guy, a normal grandfather," May said. When Mary died, John moved in with his brother, Gordon, before dying in 1997.

Gordon Wolf was a fantastic athlete as a teenager and young adult. As a freshman at Wauwatosa High School, he was already considered one of the better basketball players in the Milwaukee area. He went on to lead the Suburban Conference in scoring as a sophomore and become an all-conference forward for the school. He was also quite a golfer, once scoring a hole-in-one at Blue Mound Country Club in Wauwatosa. At some point, a disease cost Gordon one of his legs, and he died about two or three years before his brother. "Gordon was kind of a recluse," May said. "He had lost his leg, and he didn't come out of the house."

What happened to Arnold Yunk after the murder is unknown.

The Schumachers, meanwhile, had moved out of the Village within two years of the murder, purchasing a home at 176 West Center Street, where

Art Schumacher would live for the next forty-five years. The home was in a new subdivision, carved out of old farmland about a mile northwest of the old Armstrong house in which they had lived.

Art and Florence's daughter, Jeanette, graduated from Wauwatosa High School and married Lee Egloff. When Lee went overseas due to military duty during World War II, Jeanette moved back in with her parents, whose address had by this time been changed to 8118 Hillcrest Drive. She brought her two sons, Gerald and Brian, with her. A third son, Keith, was born after Lee returned from overseas and the family moved to Waukesha.

After a short time, Art and Florence reportedly stopped mentioning the murder, except perhaps in private. "Grandmother and Grandfather never said anything to me. It was as if it had never happened," Keith Egloff said. "Buddy or the case was never a topic of discussion in our family," adding that all he was told about it over many years probably took no more than a few minutes. Keith thinks that he still has a Christmas tree ornament that Buddy made for Jeanette.

"Mother pointed out to me one Christmas in the 1960s an old nicely woven small two-colored paper envelope with a handle, an item that Buddy had made," Keith said. "She, herself, would always place the envelope on the tree, hanging by its handle. At first when I was young, before she told me that Buddy had made it, I wondered why she always placed such an old, drab-looking envelope on the brightly lit and shining Christmas tree."

Brian and Keith Egloff both said that Florence was so saddened by Buddy's death that she and Art took in a nephew named Gaylord and treated him just as if he were her own son. "I often wonder how does one heal such a deep wound as losing a son," Brian Egloff said.

Art and Florence remained in the house together until Florence died in 1961, some time after having a stroke. Eight years later, Art sold the house on Hillcrest Drive to Ray Hoffman and family and moved into the Lutheran Home for the Aging in Wauwatosa for the final seven years of his life. The nursing home stands across the street from Wauwatosa Cemetery, Buddy's final resting place, and now the resting place of his parents, too.

There are many who remembered, decades later, though. In a possible reference to the Schumacher boy, Erik Groessl, who attended Lincoln School in the late 1960s, recalled that he'd been told that the ghost of a boy who had been murdered was living on the roof of the school. If someone hit a baseball or softball on the roof, the boy would decide whether to throw it back down or not.

Lillian Harwood spoke of it, too. Now I wish I had asked her who did it. Maybe she really did know who killed the Schumacher boy.

ABOUT THE AUTHOR

Paul Hoffman was born in Madison, Wisconsin, and was raised in Wauwatosa, a suburb of Milwaukee. He is a 1981 graduate of Wauwatosa East High School and attended both the University of Wisconsin–Madison and the University of Wisconsin–Milwaukee, graduating in 1985 with a bachelor's degree in mass communications (radio/TV) and a minor in English.

His nearly thirty-year career in journalism consists of working as a sportswriter at the *Milwaukee Sentinel*; assistant sports editor at Pioneer Press newspapers in the Chicago area; sports editor and news editor in Shelbyville, Indiana; and news editor in Columbus, Indiana. He has also been special publications editor at the *Daily Journal* in Franklin, Indiana, since 2001.

Paul is a member of the Wauwatosa, Milwaukee County and Wisconsin Historical Societies.

He is married and has three daughters, a son and two stepdaughters.

He is still researching this case and open to receiving new information on the people and circumstances involved. If you can help, please contact him at PO Box 2611, Columbus, Indiana, 47201, via e-mail at phof63@sbcglobal.net or at the website PaulHoffmanAuthor.com.